OUR TOWN

OUR TOWN

A Play in Three Acts

THORNTON WILDER

THIS EDITION INCLUDES THORNTON WILDER'S
ESSAY "SOME THOUGHTS ON PLAYWRIGHTING"

A Perennial Classic
Harper & Row, Publishers
New York

OUR TOWN

Copyright © 1938, 1957 by Thornton Wilder

Printed in the United States of America

First PERENNIAL CLASSIC *edition published 1968 by Harper & Row, Publishers, Inc., New York, N.Y.10022.*

Library of Congress catalog card number: 60-16885

To Alexander Woollcott
of Castleton Township, Rutland County, Vermont

OUR TOWN

CHARACTERS (in the order of their appearance)

STAGE MANAGER
DR. GIBBS
JOE CROWELL
HOWIE NEWSOME
MRS. GIBBS
MRS. WEBB
GEORGE GIBBS
REBECCA GIBBS
WALLY WEBB
EMILY WEBB
PROFESSOR WILLARD
MR. WEBB
WOMAN IN THE BALCONY
MAN IN THE AUDITORIUM
LADY IN THE BOX
SIMON STIMSON
MRS. SOAMES
CONSTABLE WARREN
SI CROWELL
THREE BASEBALL PLAYERS
SAM CRAIG
JOE STODDARD

The entire play takes place in Grover's Corners, New Hampshire.

The first performance of this play took place at the McCarter Theatre, Princeton, New Jersey, on January 22, 1938. The first New York performance was at the Henry Miller Theatre, February 4, 1938. It was produced and directed by Jed Harris. The technical director was Raymond Sovey; the costumes were designed by Madame Hélène Pons. The role of the Stage Manager was played by Frank Craven. The Gibbs family were played by Jay Fassett, Evelyn Varden, John Craven and Marilyn Erskine; the Webb family by Thomas Ross, Helen Carew, Martha Scott (as Emily) and Charles Wiley, Jr. Mrs. Soames was played by Doro Merande; Simon Stimson by Philip Coolidge.

ACT I

STAGE MANAGER:

This play is called "Our Town." It was written by Thornton Wilder; produced and directed by A. . . . (or: produced by A. . . .; directed by B. . . .). In it you will see Miss C. . . .; Miss D. . . .; Miss E. . . .; and Mr. F. . . .; Mr. G. . . .; Mr. H. . . .; and many others. The name of the town is Grover's Corners, New Hampshire—just across the Massachusetts line: latitude 42 degrees 40 minutes; longitude 70 degrees 37 minutes. The First Act shows a day in our town. The day is May 7, 1901. The time is just before dawn.

A rooster crows.

The sky is beginning to show some streaks of light over in the East there, behind our mount'in.

The morning star always gets wonderful bright the minute before it has to go,—doesn't it?

He stares at it for a moment, then goes upstage.

Well, I'd better show you how our town lies. Up here—

That is: parallel with the back wall.

is Main Street. Way back there is the railway station; tracks go that way. Polish Town's across the tracks, and some Canuck families.

Toward the left.

Over there is the Congregational Church; across the street's the Presbyterian.

Methodist and Unitarian are over there.

Baptist is down in the holla' by the river.

Catholic Church is over beyond the tracks.

Here's the Town Hall and Post Office combined; jail's in the basement.

Bryan once made a speech from these very steps here.

Along here's a row of stores. Hitching posts and horse blocks in front of them. First automobile's going to come along in about five years—belonged to Banker Cartwright, our richest citizen . . . lives in the big white house up on the hill.

Here's the grocery store and here's Mr. Morgan's drugstore. Most everybody in town manages to look into those two stores once a day.

Public School's over yonder. High School's still farther over. Quarter of nine mornings, noontimes, and three o'clock afternoons, the hull town can hear the yelling and screaming from those schoolyards.

He approaches the table and chairs downstage right.

ACT ONE

This is our doctor's house,—Doc Gibbs'. This is the back door.

> *Two arched trellises, covered with vines and flowers, are
> pushed out, one by each proscenium pillar.*

There's some scenery for those who think they have to have scenery.

This is Mrs. Gibbs' garden. Corn . . . peas . . . beans . . . hollyhocks
. . heliotrope . . . and a lot of burdock.

> *Crosses the stage.*

In those days our newspaper come out twice a week—the
Grover's Corners *Sentinel*—and this is Editor Webb's house.

And this is Mrs. Webb's garden.

Just like Mrs. Gibbs', only it's got a lot of sunflowers, too.

> *He looks upward, center stage.*

Right here . . .'s a big butternut tree.

> *He returns to his place by the right proscenium pillar and
> looks at the audience for a minute.*

Nice town, y'know what I mean?

Nobody very remarkable ever come out of it, s'far as we know.

The earliest tombstones in the cemetery up there on the mountain
say 1670-1680—they're Grovers and Cartwrights and Gibbses and
Herseys—same names as are around here now.

Well, as I said: it's about dawn.

The only lights on in town are in a cottage over by the tracks
where a Polish mother's just had twins. And in the Joe Crowell
house, where Joe Junior's getting up so as to deliver the paper.
And in the depot, where Shorty Hawkins is gettin' ready to flag
the 5:45 for Boston.

> *A train whistle is heard. The* STAGE MANAGER *takes out his
> watch and nods.*

Naturally, out in the country—all around—there've been lights on
for some time, what with milkin's and so on. But town people
sleep late.

7

So—another day's begun.

There's Doc Gibbs comin' down Main Street now, comin' back from that baby case. And here's his wife comin' downstairs to get breakfast.

> MRS. GIBBS, *a plump, pleasant woman in the middle thirties comes "downstairs" right. She pulls up an imaginary window shade in her kitchen and starts to make a fire in her stove.*

Doc Gibbs died in 1930. The new hospital's named after him.

Mrs. Gibbs died first—long time ago, in fact. She went out to visit her daughter, Rebecca, who married an insurance man in Canton, Ohio, and died there—pneumonia—but her body was brought back here. She's up in the cemetery there now—in with a whole mess of Gibbses and Herseys—she was Julia Hersey 'fore she married Doc Gibbs in the Congregational Church over there.

In our town we like to know the facts about everybody.

There's Mrs. Webb, coming downstairs to get her breakfast, too.

—That's Doc Gibbs. Got that call at half past one this morning.

And there comes Joe Crowell, Jr., delivering Mr. Webb' *Sentinel.*

> DR. GIBBS *has been coming along Main Street from the left. At the point where he would turn to approach his house he stops, sets down his—imaginary—black bag, takes off his hat, and rubs his face with fatigue, using an enormous handkerchief.*
>
> MRS. WEBB, *a thin, serious, crisp woman, has entered her kitchen, left, tying on an apron. She goes through the motions of putting wood into a stove, lighting it, and preparing breakfast.*
>
> *Suddenly,* JOE CROWELL, JR., *eleven, starts down Main Street from the right, hurling imaginary newspapers into doorways.*

8

JOE CROWELL, JR.:

Morning, Doc Gibbs.

DR. GIBBS:

Morning, Joe.

JOE CROWELL, JR.:

Somebody been sick, Doc?

DR. GIBBS:

No. Just some twins born over in Polish Town.

JOE CROWELL, JR.:

Do you want your paper now?

DR. GIBBS:

Yes, I'll take it.—Anything serious goin' on in the world since Wednesday?

JOE CROWELL, JR.:

Yessir. My schoolteacher, Miss Foster, 's getting married to a fella over in Concord.

DR. GIBBS:

I declare.—How do you boys feel about that?

JOE CROWELL, JR.:

Well, of course, it's none of my business—but I think if a person starts out to be a teacher, she ought to stay one.

DR. GIBBS:

How's your knee, Joe?

JOE CROWELL, JR.:

Fine, Doc, I never think about it at all. Only like you said, it always tells me when it's going to rain.

DR. GIBBS:

What's it telling you today? Goin' to rain?

JOE CROWELL, JR.:

No, sir.

DR. GIBBS:

Sure?

JOE CROWELL, JR.:

Yessir.

DR. GIBBS:

Knee ever make a mistake?

JOE CROWELL, JR.:

No, sir.

> JOE *goes off.* DR. GIBBS *stands reading his paper.*

STAGE MANAGER:

Want to tell you something about that boy Joe Crowell there. Joe was awful bright—graduated from high school here, head of his class. So he got a scholarship to Massachusetts Tech. Graduated head of his class there, too. It was all wrote up in the Boston paper at the time. Goin' to be a great engineer, Joe was. But the war broke out and he died in France.—All that education for nothing.

HOWIE NEWSOME:

> *Off left.*

Giddap, Bessie! What's the matter with you today?

STAGE MANAGER:

Here comes Howie Newsome, deliverin' the milk.

> HOWIE NEWSOME, *about thirty, in overalls, comes along Main Street from the left, walking beside an invisible horse*

and wagon and carrying an imaginary rack with milk bottles. The sound of clinking milk bottles is heard. He leaves some bottles at Mrs. Webb's trellis, then, crossing the stage to Mrs. Gibbs', he stops center to talk to Dr. Gibbs.

HOWIE NEWSOME:

Morning, Doc.

DR. GIBBS:

Morning, Howie.

HOWIE NEWSOME:

Somebody sick?

DR. GIBBS:

Pair of twins over to Mrs. Goruslawski's.

HOWIE NEWSOME:

Twins, eh? This town's gettin' bigger every year.

DR. GIBBS:

Goin' to rain, Howie?

HOWIE NEWSOME:

No, no. Fine day—that'll burn through. Come on, Bessie.

DR. GIBBS:

Hello Bessie.
        He strokes the horse, which has remained up center.
How old is she, Howie?

HOWIE NEWSOME:

Going on seventeen. Bessie's all mixed up about the route ever since the Lockharts stopped takin' their quart of milk every day. She wants to leave 'em a quart just the same—keeps scolding me the hull trip.

> *He reaches Mrs. Gibbs' back door. She is waiting for him.*

MRS. GIBBS:

Good morning, Howie.

HOWIE NEWSOME:

Morning, Mrs. Gibbs. Doc's just comin' down the street.

MRS. GIBBS:

Is he? Seems like you're late today.

HOWIE NEWSOME:

Yes. Somep'n went wrong with the separator. Don't know what 'twas.

> *He passes Dr. Gibbs up center.*

Doc!

DR. GIBBS:

Howie!

MRS. GIBBS:

> *Calling upstairs.*

Children! Children! Time to get up.

HOWIE NEWSOME:

Come on, Bessie!

> *He goes off right.*

MRS. GIBBS:

George! Rebecca!

> DR. GIBBS *arrives at his back door and passes through the trellis into his house.*

MRS. GIBBS:

Everything all right, Frank?

DR. GIBBS:

Yes. I declare—easy as kittens.

MRS. GIBBS:

Bacon'll be ready in a minute. Set down and drink your coffee. You can catch a couple hours' sleep this morning, can't you?

DR. GIBBS:

Hm! . . . Mrs. Wentworth's coming at eleven. Guess I know what it's about, too. Her stummick ain't what it ought to be.

MRS. GIBBS:

All told, you won't get more'n three hours' sleep. Frank Gibbs, I don't know what's goin' to become of you. I do wish I could get you to go away someplace and take a rest. I think it would do you good.

MRS. WEBB:

Emileeee! Time to get up! Wally! Seven o'clock!

MRS. GIBBS:

I declare, you got to speak to George. Seems like something's come over him lately. He's no help to me at all. I can't even get him to cut me some wood.

DR. GIBBS:

> *Washing and drying his hands at the sink.* MRS. GIBBS *is busy at the stove.*

Is he sassy to you?

MRS. GIBBS:

No. He just whines! All he thinks about is that baseball— George! Rebecca! You'll be late for school.

DR. GIBBS:

M-m-m . . .

MRS. GIBBS:

George!

DR. GIBBS:

George, look sharp!

GEORGE'S VOICE:

Yes, Pa!

DR. GIBBS:

As he goes off the stage.

Don't you hear your mother calling you? I guess I'll go upstairs and get forty winks.

MRS. WEBB:

Walleee! Emileee! You'll be late for school! Walleee! You wash yourself good or I'll come up and do it myself.

REBECCA GIBBS' VOICE:

Ma! What dress shall I wear?

MRS. GIBBS:

Don't make a noise. Your father's been out all night and needs his sleep. I washed and ironed the blue gingham for you special.

REBECCA:

Ma, I hate that dress.

MRS. GIBBS:

Oh, hush-up-with-you.

REBECCA:

Every day I go to school dressed like a sick turkey.

MRS. GIBBS:

Now, Rebecca, you always look *very* nice.

REBECCA:

Mama, George's throwing soap at me.

MRS. GIBBS:

I'll come and slap the both of you,—that's what I'll do.

> *A factory whistle sounds.*
>
> *The* CHILDREN *dash in and take their places at the tables. Right,* GEORGE, *about sixteen, and* REBECCA, *eleven. Left,* EMILY *and* WALLY, *same ages. They carry strapped school-books.*

STAGE MANAGER:

We've got a factory in our town too—hear it? Makes blankets. Cartwrights own it and it brung 'em a fortune.

MRS. WEBB:

Children! Now I won't have it. Breakfast is just as good as any other meal and I won't have you gobbling like wolves. It'll stunt your growth,—that's a fact. Put away your book, Wally.

WALLY:

Aw, Ma! By ten o'clock I got to know all about Canada.

MRS. WEBB:

You know the rule's well as I do—no books at table. As for me, I'd rather have my children healthy than bright.

EMILY:

I'm both, Mama: you know I am. I'm the brightest girl in school for my age. I have a wonderful memory.

MRS. WEBB:

Eat your breakfast.

WALLY:

I'm bright, too, when I'm looking at my stamp collection.

MRS. GIBBS:

I'll speak to your father about it when he's rested. Seems to me twenty-five cents a week's enough for a boy your age. I declare I don't know how you spend it all.

GEORGE:

Aw, Ma,—I gotta lotta things to buy.

MRS. GIBBS:

Strawberry phosphates—that's what you spend it on.

GEORGE:

I don't see how Rebecca comes to have so much money. She has more'n a dollar.

REBECCA:

> *Spoon in mouth, dreamily.*

I've been saving it up gradual.

MRS. GIBBS:

Well, dear, I think it's a good thing to spend some every now and then.

REBECCA:

Mama, do you know what I love most in the world—do you?—Money.

MRS. GIBBS:

Eat your breakfast.

THE CHILDREN:

Mama, there's first bell.—I gotta hurry.—I don't want any more.—I gotta hurry.

> *The* CHILDREN *rise, seize their books and dash out through*

the trellises. They meet, down center, and chattering, walk to Main Street, then turn left.

The STAGE MANAGER goes off, unobtrusively, right.

MRS. WEBB:

Walk fast, but you don't have to run. Wally, pull up your pants at the knee. Stand up straight, Emily.

MRS. GIBBS:

Tell Miss Foster I send her my best congratulations—can you remember that?

REBECCA:

Yes, Ma.

MRS. GIBBS:

You look real nice, Rebecca. Pick up your feet.

ALL:

Good-by.

> MRS. GIBBS *fills her apron with food for the chickens and comes down to the footlights.*

MRS. GIBBS:

Here, chick, chick, chick.

No, go away, you. Go away.

Here, chick, chick, chick.

What's the matter with *you?* Fight, fight, fight,—that's all you do.

Hm . . . *you* don't belong to me. Where'd you come from?

> *She shakes her apron.*

Oh, don't be so scared. Nobody's going to hurt you.

> MRS. WEBB *is sitting on the bench by her trellis, stringing beans.*

Good morning, Myrtle. How's your cold?

MRS. WEBB:

Well, I still get that tickling feeling in my throat. I told Charles I didn't know as I'd go to choir practice tonight. Wouldn't be any use.

MRS. GIBBS:

Have you tried singing over your voice?

MRS. WEBB:

Yes, but somehow I can't do that and stay on the key. While I'm resting myself I thought I'd string some of these beans.

MRS. GIBBS:

    Rolling up her sleeves as she crosses the stage for a chat.
Let me help you. Beans have been good this year.

MRS. WEBB:

I've decided to put up forty quarts if it kills me. The children say they hate 'em, but I notice they're able to get 'em down all winter.
    Pause. Brief sound of chickens cackling.

MRS. GIBBS:

Now, Myrtle. I've got to tell you something, because if I don't tell somebody I'll burst.

MRS. WEBB:

Why, Julia Gibbs!

MRS. GIBBS:

Here, give me some more of those beans. Myrtle, did one of those secondhand-furniture men from Boston come to see you last Friday?

MRS. WEBB:

No-o.

MRS. GIBBS:

Well, he called on me. First I thought he was a patient wantin' to see Dr. Gibbs. 'N he wormed his way into my parlor, and, Myrtle Webb, he offered me three hundred and fifty dollars for Grandmother Wentworth's highboy, as I'm sitting here!

MRS. WEBB:

Why, Julia Gibbs!

MRS. GIBBS:

He did! That old thing! Why, it was so big I didn't know where to put it and I almost give it to Cousin Hester Wilcox.

MRS. WEBB:

Well, you're going to take it, aren't you?

MRS. GIBBS:

I don't know.

MRS. WEBB:

You don't know—three hundred and fifty dollars! What's come over you?

MRS. GIBBS:

Well, if I could get the Doctor to take the money and go away someplace on a real trip, I'd sell it like that.—Y'know, Myrtle, it's been the dream of my life to see Paris, France.—Oh, I don't know. It sounds crazy, I suppose, but for years I've been promising myself that if we ever had the chance—

MRS. WEBB:

How does the Doctor feel about it?

MRS. GIBBS:

Well, I did beat about the bush a little and said that if I got a legacy—that's the way I put it—I'd make him take me somewhere.

MRS. WEBB:

M-m-m . . . What did he say?

MRS. GIBBS:

You know how he is. I haven't heard a serious word out of him since I've known him. No, he said, it might make him discontented with Grover's Corners to go traipsin' about Europe; better let well enough alone, he says. Every two years he makes a trip to the battlefields of the Civil War and that's enough treat for anybody, he says.

MRS. WEBB:

Well, Mr. Webb just *admires* the way Dr. Gibbs knows everything about the Civil War. Mr. Webb's a good mind to give up Napoleon and move over to the Civil War, only Dr. Gibbs being one of the greatest experts in the country just makes him despair.

MRS. GIBBS:

It's a fact! Dr. Gibbs is never so happy as when he's at Antietam or Gettysburg. The times I've walked over those hills, Myrtle, stopping at every bush and pacing it all out, like we were going to buy it.

MRS. WEBB:

Well, if that secondhand man's really serious about buyin' it, Julia, you sell it. And then you'll get to see Paris, all right. Just keep droppin' hints from time to time—that's how I got to see the Atlantic Ocean, y'know.

MRS. GIBBS:

Oh, I'm sorry I mentioned it. Only it seems to me that once in your life before you die you ought to see a country where they don't talk in English and don't even want to.

> *The* STAGE MANAGER *enters briskly from the right. He tips his hat to the ladies, who nod their heads.*

STAGE MANAGER:

Thank you, ladies. Thank you very much.

> MRS. GIBBS *and* MRS. WEBB *gather up their things, return into their homes and disappear.*

Now we're going to skip a few hours.

But first we want a little more information about the town, kind of a scientific account, you might say.

So I've asked Professor Willard of our State University to sketch in a few details of our past history here.

Is Professor Willard here?

> PROFESSOR WILLARD, *a rural savant, pince-nez on a wide satin ribbon, enters from the right with some notes in his hand.*

May I introduce Professor Willard of our State University.

A few brief notes, thank you, Professor,—unfortunately our time is limited.

PROFESSOR WILLARD:

Grover's Corners . . . let me see . . . Grover's Corners lies on the old Pleistocene granite of the Appalachian range. I may say it's some of the oldest land in the world. We're very proud of that. A shelf of Devonian basalt crosses it with vestiges of Mesozoic shale, and some sandstone outcroppings; but that's all more recent: two hundred, three hundred million years old.

Some highly interesting fossils have been found . . . I may say: unique fossils . . . two miles out of town, in Silas Peckham's cow pasture. They can be seen at the museum in our University at any time—that is, at any reasonable time. Shall I read some of Professor Gruber's notes on the meteorological situation—mean precipitation, et cetera?

STAGE MANAGER:

Afraid we won't have time for that, Professor. We might have a few words on the history of man here.

PROFESSOR WILLARD:

Yes . . . anthropological data: Early Amerindian stock. Cotahatchee tribes . . . no evidence before the tenth century of this era . . . hm . . . now entirely disappeared . . . possible traces in three families. Migration toward the end of the seventeenth century of English brachiocephalic blue-eyed stock . . . for the most part. Since then some Slav and Mediterranean—

STAGE MANAGER:

And the population, Professor Willard?

PROFESSOR WILLARD:

Within the town limits: 2,640.

STAGE MANAGER:

Just a moment, Professor.
> *He whispers into the professor's ear.*

PROFESSOR WILLARD:

Oh, yes, indeed?—The population, *at the moment*, is 2,642. The Postal District brings in 507 more, making a total of 3,149.—Mortality and birth rates: constant.—By MacPherson's gauge: 6.032.

STAGE MANAGER:

Thank you very much, Professor. We're all very much obliged to you, I'm sure.

PROFESSOR WILLARD:

Not at all, sir; not at all.

STAGE MANAGER:

This way, Professor, and thank you again.
> *Exit* PROFESSOR WILLARD.

Now the political and social report: Editor Webb.—Oh, Mr. Webb?

MRS. WEBB *appears at her back door.*

MRS. WEBB:

He'll be here in a minute. . . . He just cut his hand while he was eatin' an apple.

STAGE MANAGER:

Thank you, Mrs. Webb.

MRS. WEBB:

Charles! Everybody's waitin'.

Exit MRS. WEBB.

STAGE MANAGER:

Mr. Webb is Publisher and Editor of the Grover's Corners *Sentinel.* That's our local paper, y'know.

MR. WEBB *enters from his house, pulling on his coat. His finger is bound in a handkerchief.*

MR. WEBB:

Well . . . I don't have to tell you that we're run here by a Board of Selectmen.—All males vote at the age of twenty-one. Women vote indirect. We're lower middle class: sprinkling of professional men . . . ten per cent illiterate laborers. Politically, we're eighty-six per cent Republicans; six per cent Democrats; four per cent Socialists; rest, indifferent.

Religiously, we're eighty-five per cent Protestants; twelve per cent Catholics; rest, indifferent.

STAGE MANAGER:

Have you any comments, Mr. Webb?

MR. WEBB:

Very ordinary town, if you ask me. Little better behaved than most. Probably a lot duller.

But our young people here seem to like it well enough. Ninety per cent of 'em graduating from high school settle down right here to live—even when they've been away to college.

STAGE MANAGER:

Now, is there anyone in the audience who would like to ask Editor Webb anything about the town?

WOMAN IN THE BALCONY:

Is there much drinking in Grover's Corners?

MR. WEBB:

Well, ma'am, I wouldn't know what you'd call *much*. Satiddy nights the farmhands meet down in Ellery Greenough's stable and holler some. We've got one or two town drunks, but they're always having remorses every time an evangelist comes to town. No, ma'am, I'd say likker ain't a regular thing in the home here except in the medicine chest. Right good for snake bite, y'know—always was.

BELLIGERENT MAN AT BACK OF AUDITORIUM:

Is there no one in town aware of—

STAGE MANAGER:

Come forward, will you, where we can all hear you—What were you saying?

BELLIGERENT MAN:

Is there no one in town aware of social injustice and industrial inequality?

MR. WEBB:

Oh, yes, everybody is—somethin' terrible. Seems like they spend most of their time talking about who's rich and who's poor.

BELLIGERENT MAN:

Then why don't they do something about it?
He withdraws without waiting for an answer.

MR. WEBB:

Well, I dunno. . . . I guess we're all hunting like everybody else for a way the diligent and sensible can rise to the top and the lazy and quarrelsome can sink to the bottom. But it ain't easy to find. Meanwhile, we do all we can to help those that can't help themselves and those that can we leave alone.—Are there any other questions?

LADY IN A BOX:

Oh, Mr. Webb? Mr. Webb, is there any culture or love of beauty in Grover's Corners?

MR. WEBB:

Well, ma'am, there ain't much—not in the sense you mean. Come to think of it, there's some girls that play the piano at High School Commencement; but they ain't happy about it. No, ma'am, there isn't much culture; but maybe this is the place to tell you that we've got a lot of pleasures of a kind here: we like the sun comin' up over the mountain in the morning, and we all notice a good deal about the birds. We pay a lot of attention to them. And we watch the change of the seasons; yes, everybody knows about them. But those other things—you're right, ma'am,—there ain't much.—*Robinson Crusoe* and the Bible; and Handel's "Largo," we all know that; and Whistler's "Mother"—those are just about as far as we go.

LADY IN A BOX:

So I thought. Thank you, Mr. Webb.

STAGE MANAGER:

Thank you, Mr. Webb.

> MR. WEBB *retires.*

Now, we'll go back to the town. It's early afternoon. All 2,642 have had their dinners and all the dishes have been washed.

> MR. WEBB, *having removed his coat, returns and starts pushing a lawn mower to and fro beside his house.*

There's an early-afternoon calm in our town: a buzzin' and a hummin' from the school buildings; only a few buggies on Main Street—the horses dozing at the hitching posts; you all remember what it's like. Doc Gibbs is in his office, tapping people and making them say "ah." Mr. Webb's cuttin' his lawn over there; one man in ten thinks it's a privilege to push his own lawn mower.

No, sir. It's later than I thought. There are the children coming home from school already.

> *Shrill girls' voices are heard, off left.* EMILY *comes along Main Street, carrying some books. There are some signs that she is imagining herself to be a lady of startling elegance.*

EMILY:

I *can't*, Lois. I've got to go home and help my mother. I *promised.*

MR. WEBB:

Emily, walk simply. Who do you think you are today?

EMILY:

Papa, you're terrible. One minute you tell me to stand up straight and the next minute you call me names. I just don't listen to you.

> *She gives him an abrupt kiss.*

MR. WEBB:

Golly, I never got a kiss from such a great lady before.

> *He goes out of sight.* EMILY *leans over and picks some flowers by the gate of her house.*
>
> GEORGE GIBBS *comes careening down Main Street. He is throwing a ball up to dizzying heights, and waiting to catch it again. This sometimes requires his taking six steps backward. He bumps into an* OLD LADY *invisible to us.*

GEORGE:

Excuse me, Mrs. Forrest.

STAGE MANAGER:

> *As Mrs. Forrest.*

Go out and play in the fields, young man. You got no business playing baseball on Main Street.

GEORGE:

Awfully sorry, Mrs. Forrest.—Hello, Emily.

EMILY:

H'lo.

GEORGE:

You made a fine speech in class.

EMILY:

Well . . . I was really ready to make a speech about the Monroe Doctrine, but at the last minute Miss Corcoran made me talk about the Louisiana Purchase instead. I worked an awful long time on both of them.

GEORGE:

Gee, it's funny, Emily. From my window up there I can just see your head nights when you're doing your homework over in your room.

EMILY:

Why, can you?

GEORGE:

You certainly do stick to it, Emily. I don't see how you can sit still that long. I guess you like school.

EMILY:

Well, I always feel it's something you have to go through.

GEORGE:

Yeah.

EMILY:

I don't mind it really. It passes the time.

GEORGE:

Yeah.—Emily, what do you think? We might work out a kinda telegraph from your window to mine; and once in a while you could give me a kinda hint or two about one of those algebra problems. I don't mean the answers, Emily, of course not . . . just some little hint . . .

EMILY:

Oh, I think *hints* are allowed.—So—ah—if you get stuck, George, you whistle to me; and I'll give you some hints.

GEORGE:

Emily, you're just naturally bright, I guess.

EMILY:

I figure that it's just the way a person's born.

GEORGE:

Yeah. But, you see, I want to be a farmer, and my Uncle Luke says whenever I'm ready I can come over and work on his farm and if I'm any good I can just gradually have it.

EMILY:

You mean the house and everything?

> *Enter* MRS. WEBB *with a large bowl and sits on the bench by her trellis.*

GEORGE:

Yeah. Well, thanks . . . I better be getting out to the baseball field. Thanks for the talk, Emily.—Good afternoon, Mrs. Webb.

MRS. WEBB:

Good afternoon, George.

GEORGE:

So long, Emily.

EMILY:

So long, George.

MRS. WEBB:

Emily, come and help me string these beans for the winter. George Gibbs let himself have a real conversation, didn't he? Why, he's growing up. How old would George be?

EMILY:

I don't know.

MRS. WEBB:

Let's see. He must be almost sixteen.

EMILY:

Mama, I made a speech in class today and I was very good.

MRS. WEBB:

You must recite it to your father at supper. What was it about?

EMILY:

The Louisiana Purchase. It was like silk off a spool. I'm going to make speeches all my life.—Mama, are these big enough?

MRS. WEBB:

Try and get them a little bigger if you can.

EMILY:

Mama, will you answer me a question, serious?

MRS. WEBB:

Seriously, dear—not serious.

EMILY:

Seriously,—will you?

MRS. WEBB:

Of course, I will.

EMILY:

Mama, am I good looking?

MRS. WEBB:

Yes, of course you are. All my children have got good features; I'd be ashamed if they hadn't.

EMILY:

Oh, Mama, that's not what I mean. What I mean is: am I *pretty?*

MRS. WEBB:

I've already told you, yes. Now that's enough of that. You have a nice young pretty face. I never heard of such foolishness.

ACT ONE

EMILY:

Oh, Mama, you never tell us the truth about anything.

MRS. WEBB:

I *am* telling you the truth.

EMILY:

Mama, were *you* pretty?

MRS. WEBB:

Yes, I was, if I do say it. I was the prettiest girl in town next to Mamie Cartwright.

EMILY:

But, Mama, you've got to say *some*thing about me. Am I pretty enough . . . to get anybody . . . to get people interested in me?

MRS. WEBB:

Emily, you make me tired. Now stop it. You're pretty enough for all normal purposes.—Come along now and bring that bowl with you.

EMILY:

Oh, Mama, you're no help at all.

STAGE MANAGER:

Thank you. Thank you! That'll do. We'll have to interrupt again here. Thank you, Mrs. Webb; thank you, Emily.

> MRS. WEBB *and* EMILY *withdraw.*

There are some more things we want to explore about this town.

> *He comes to the center of the stage. During the following speech the lights gradually dim to darkness, leaving only a spot on him.*

I think this is a good time to tell you that the Cartwright interests have just begun building a new bank in Grover's Corners—had to go to Vermont for the marble, sorry to say. And they've asked a friend of mine what they should put in the cornerstone for people to dig up . . . a thousand years from now. . . . Of course, they've put in a copy of the *New York Times* and a copy of Mr. Webb's *Sentinel*. . . . We're kind of interested in this because some scientific fellas have found a way of painting all that reading matter with a glue—a silicate glue—that'll make it keep a thousand—two thousand years.

We're putting in a Bible . . . and the Constitution of the United States—and a copy of William Shakespeare's plays. What do you say, folks? What do you think?

Y'know—Babylon once had two million people in it, and all we know about 'em is the names of the kings and some copies of wheat contracts . . . and contracts for the sale of slaves. Yet every night all those families sat down to supper, and the father came home from his work, and the smoke went up the chimney,—same as here. And even in Greece and Rome, all we know about the *real* life of the people is what we can piece together out of the joking poems and the comedies they wrote for the theatre back then.

So I'm going to have a copy of this play put in the cornerstone and the people a thousand years from now'll know a few simple facts about us—more than the Treaty of Versailles and the Lindbergh flight.

See what I mean?

So—people a thousand years from now—this is the way we were in the provinces north of New York at the beginning of the twentieth century.—This is the way we were: in our growing up and in our marrying and in our living and in our dying.

> *A choir partially concealed in the orchestra pit has begun singing "Blessed Be the Tie That Binds."*

SIMON STIMSON *stands directing them.*

Two ladders have been pushed onto the stage; they serve as indication of the second story in the Gibbs and Webb houses. GEORGE *and* EMILY *mount them, and apply themselves to their schoolwork.*

DR. GIBBS *has entered and is seated in his kitchen reading.*

Well!—good deal of time's gone by. It's evening.

You can hear choir practice going on in the Congregational Church.

The children are at home doing their schoolwork.

The day's running down like a tired clock.

SIMON STIMSON:

Now look here, everybody. Music come into the world to give pleasure.—Softer! Softer! Get it out of your heads that music's only good when it's loud. You leave loudness to the Methodists. You couldn't beat 'em, even if you wanted to. Now again. Tenors!

GEORGE:

Hssst! Emily!

EMILY:

Hello.

GEORGE:

Hello!

EMILY:

I can't work at all. The moonlight's so *terrible.*

GEORGE:

Emily, did you get the third problem?

EMILY:

Which?

GEORGE:

The *third?*

EMILY:

Why, yes, George—that's the easiest of them all.

GEORGE:

I don't see it. Emily, can you give me a hint?

EMILY:

I'll tell you one thing: the answer's in yards.

GEORGE:

! ! ! In yards? How do you mean?

EMILY:

In *square* yards.

GEORGE:

Oh . . . in square yards.

EMILY:

Yes, George, don't you see?

GEORGE:

Yeah.

EMILY:

In square yards of *wallpaper*.

GEORGE:

Wallpaper,—oh, I see. Thanks a lot, Emily.

EMILY:

You're welcome. My, isn't the moonlight *terrible?* And choir practice going on.—I think if you hold your breath you can hear the train all the way to Contoocook. Hear it?

GEORGE:

M-m-m—What do you know!

EMILY:

Well, I guess I better go back and try to work.

GEORGE:

Good night, Emily. And thanks.

EMILY:

Good night, George.

SIMON STIMSON:

Before I forget it: how many of you will be able to come in Tuesday afternoon and sing at Fred Hersey's wedding?—show your hands. That'll be fine; that'll be right nice. We'll do the same music we did for Jane Trowbridge's last month.
—Now we'll do: "Art Thou Weary; Art Thou Languid?" It's a question, ladies and gentlemen, make it talk. Ready.

DR. GIBBS:

Oh, George, can you come down a minute?

GEORGE:

Yes, Pa.
> *He descends the ladder.*

DR. GIBBS:

Make yourself comfortable, George; I'll only keep you a minute. George, how old are you?

GEORGE:

I? I'm sixteen, almost seventeen.

DR. GIBBS:

What do you want to do after school's over?

GEORGE:

Why, you know, Pa. I want to be a farmer on Uncle Luke's farm.

DR. GIBBS:

You'll be willing, will you, to get up early and milk and feed the stock . . . and you'll be able to hoe and hay all day?

GEORGE:

Sure, I will. What are you . . . what do you mean, Pa?

DR. GIBBS:

Well, George, while I was in my office today I heard a funny sound . . . and what do you think it was? It was your mother chopping wood. There you see your mother—getting up early; cooking meals all day long; washing and ironing;—and still she has to go out in the back yard and chop wood. I suppose she just got tired of asking you. She just gave up and decided it was easier to do it herself. And you eat her meals, and put on the clothes she keeps nice for you, and you run off and play baseball,—like she's some hired girl we keep around the house but that we don't like very much. Well, I knew all I had to do was call your attention to it. Here's a handkerchief, son. George, I've decided to raise your spending money twenty-five cents a week. Not, of course, for chopping wood for your mother, because that's a present you give her, but because you're getting older—and I imagine there are lots of things you must find to do with it.

GEORGE:

Thanks, Pa.

DR. GIBBS:

Let's see—tomorrow's your payday. You can count on it—Hmm. Probably Rebecca'll feel she ought to have some more too. Wonder what could have happened to your mother. Choir practice never was as late as this before.

GEORGE:

It's only half past eight, Pa.

DR. GIBBS:

I don't know why she's in that old choir. She hasn't any more voice than an old crow. . . . Traipsin' around the streets at this hour of the night . . . Just about time you retired, don't you think?

GEORGE:

Yes, Pa.

> GEORGE *mounts to his place on the ladder.*
> *Laughter and good nights can be heard on stage left and presently* MRS. GIBBS, MRS. SOAMES *and* MRS. WEBB *come down Main Street. When they arrive at the corner of the stage they stop.*

MRS. SOAMES:

Good night, Martha. Good night, Mr. Foster.

MRS. WEBB:

I'll tell Mr. Webb; I *know* he'll want to put it in the paper.

MRS. GIBBS:

My, it's late!

MRS. SOAMES:

Good night, Irma.

MRS. GIBBS:

Real nice choir practice, wa'n't it? Myrtle Webb! Look at that moon, will you! Tsk-tsk-tsk. Potato weather, for sure.

They are silent a moment, gazing up at the moon.

MRS. SOAMES:

Naturally I didn't want to say a word about it in front of those others, but now we're alone—really, it's the worst scandal that ever was in this town!

MRS. GIBBS:

What?

MRS. SOAMES:

Simon Stimson!

MRS. GIBBS:

Now, Louella!

MRS. SOAMES:

But, Julia! To have the organist of a church *drink* and *drunk* year after year. You know he was drunk tonight.

MRS. GIBBS:

Now, Louella! We all know about Mr. Stimson, and we all know about the troubles he's been through, and Dr. Ferguson knows too, and if Dr. Ferguson keeps him on there in his job the only thing the rest of us can do is just not to notice it.

MRS. SOAMES:

Not to notice it! But it's getting worse.

MRS. WEBB:

No, it isn't, Louella. It's getting better. I've been in that choir twice as long as you have. It doesn't happen anywhere near so often. . . . My, I hate to go to bed on a night like this.—I better hurry. Those children'll be sitting up till all hours. Good night, Louella.

> *They all exchange good nights. She hurries downstage, enters her house and disappears.*

MRS. GIBBS:

Can you get home safe, Louella?

MRS. SOAMES:

It's as bright as day. I can see Mr. Soames scowling at the window now. You'd think we'd been to a dance the way the menfolk carry on.

> *More good nights.* MRS. GIBBS *arrives at her home and passes through the trellis into the kitchen.*

MRS. GIBBS:

Well, we had a real good time.

DR. GIBBS:

You're late enough.

MRS. GIBBS:

Why, Frank, it ain't any later 'n usual.

DR. GIBBS:

And you stopping at the corner to gossip with a lot of hens.

MRS. GIBBS:

Now, Frank, don't be grouchy. Come out and smell the heliotrope in the moonlight.

> *They stroll out arm in arm along the footlights.*

Isn't that wonderful? What did you do all the time I was away?

DR. GIBBS:

Oh, I read—as usual. What were the girls gossiping about to-night?

MRS. GIBBS:

Well, believe me, Frank—there is something to gossip about.

DR. GIBBS:

Hmm! Simon Stimson far gone, was he?

MRS. GIBBS:

Worst I've ever seen him. How'll that end, Frank? Dr. Ferguson can't forgive him forever.

DR. GIBBS:

I guess I know more about Simon Stimson's affairs than anybody in this town. Some people ain't made for small-town life. I don't know how that'll end; but there's nothing we can do but just leave it alone. Come, get in.

MRS. GIBBS:

No, not yet . . . Frank, I'm worried about you.

DR. GIBBS:

What are you worried about?

MRS. GIBBS:

I think it's my duty to make plans for you to get a real rest and change. And if I get that legacy, well, I'm going to insist on it.

DR. GIBBS:

Now, Julia, there's no sense in going over that again.

MRS. GIBBS:

Frank, you're just *unreasonable!*

DR. GIBBS:

> *Starting into the house.*

Come on, Julia, it's getting late. First thing you know you'll catch cold. I gave George a piece of my mind tonight. I reckon you'll have your wood chopped for a while anyway. No, no, start getting upstairs.

MRS. GIBBS:

Oh, dear. There's always so many things to pick up, seems like. You know, Frank, Mrs. Fairchild always locks her front door every night. All those people up that part of town do.

DR. GIBBS:

> *Blowing out the lamp.*

They're all getting citified, that's the trouble with them. They haven't got nothing fit to burgle and everybody knows it.

> *They disappear.*

> REBECCA *climbs up the ladder beside* GEORGE.

GEORGE:

Get out, Rebecca. There's only room for one at this window. You're always spoiling everything.

REBECCA:

Well, let me look just a minute.

GEORGE:

Use your own window.

REBECCA:

I did, but there's no moon there. . . . George, do you know what I think, do you? I think maybe the moon's getting nearer and nearer and there'll be a big 'splosion.

GEORGE:

Rebecca, you don't know anything. If the moon were getting nearer, the guys that sit up all night with telescopes would see it first and they'd tell about it, and it'd be in all the newspapers.

REBECCA:

George, is the moon shining on South America, Canada and half the whole world?

GEORGE:

Well—prob'ly is.

> The STAGE MANAGER *strolls on.*
> *Pause. The sound of crickets is heard.*

STAGE MANAGER:

Nine thirty. Most of the lights are out. No, there's Constable Warren trying a few doors on Main Street. And here comes Editor Webb, after putting his newspaper to bed.

> MR. WARREN, *an elderly policeman, comes along Main Street from the right,* MR. WEBB *from the left.*

MR. WEBB:

Good evening, Bill.

CONSTABLE WARREN:

Evenin', Mr. Webb.

MR. WEBB:

Quite a moon!

CONSTABLE WARREN:

Yepp.

MR. WEBB:

All quiet tonight?

ACT ONE

CONSTABLE WARREN:

Simon Stimson is rollin' around a little. Just saw his wife movin' out to hunt for him so I looked the other way—there he is now.

> SIMON STIMSON *comes down Main Street from the left, only a trace of unsteadiness in his walk.*

MR. WEBB:

Good evening, Simon . . . Town seems to have settled down for the night pretty well. . . .

> SIMON STIMSON *comes up to him and pauses a moment and stares at him, swaying slightly.*

Good evening . . . Yes, most of the town's settled down for the night, Simon. . . . I guess we better do the same. Can I walk along a ways with you?

> SIMON STIMSON *continues on his way without a word and disappears at the right.*

Good night.

CONSTABLE WARREN:

I don't know how that's goin' to end, Mr. Webb.

MR. WEBB:

Well, he's seen a peck of trouble, one thing after another. . . . Oh, Bill . . . if you see my boy smoking cigarettes, just give him a word, will you? He thinks a lot of you, Bill.

CONSTABLE WARREN:

I don't think he smokes no cigarettes, Mr. Webb. Leastways, not more'n two or three a year.

MR. WEBB:

Hm . . . I hope not.—Well, good night, Bill.

CONSTABLE WARREN:

Good night, Mr. Webb.
> *Exit.*

MR. WEBB:

Who's that up there? Is that you, Myrtle?

EMILY:

No, it's me, Papa.

MR. WEBB:

Why aren't you in bed?

EMILY:

I don't know. I just can't sleep yet, Papa. The moonlight's so *won*-derful. And the smell of Mrs. Gibbs' heliotrope. Can you smell it?

MR. WEBB:

Hm . . . Yes. Haven't any troubles on your mind, have you, Emily?

EMILY:

Troubles, Papa? *No*.

MR. WEBB:

Well, enjoy yourself, but don't let your mother catch you. Good night, Emily.

EMILY:

Good night, Papa.
> MR. WEBB *crosses into the house, whistling "Blessed Be the Tie That Binds" and disappears.*

REBECCA:

I never told you about that letter Jane Crofut got from her minister when she was sick. He wrote Jane a letter and on the envelope the address was like this: It said: Jane Crofut; The Crofut Farm; Grover's Corners; Sutton County; New Hampshire; United States of America.

GEORGE:

What's funny about that?

REBECCA:

But listen, it's not finished: the United States of America; Continent of North America; Western Hemisphere; the Earth; the Solar System; the Universe; the Mind of God—that's what it said on the envelope.

GEORGE:

What do you know!

REBECCA:

And the postman brought it just the same.

GEORGE:

What do you know!

STAGE MANAGER:

That's the end of the First Act, friends. You can go and smoke now, those that smoke.

ACT II

The tables and chairs of the two kitchens are still on the stage.
The ladders and the small bench have been withdrawn.
The STAGE MANAGER *has been at his accustomed place watching the audience return to its seats.*

STAGE MANAGER:

Three years have gone by.

Yes, the sun's come up over a thousand times.

Summers and winters have cracked the mountains a little bit more and the rains have brought down some of the dirt.

Some babies that weren't even born before have begun talking regular sentences already; and a number of people who thought they were right young and spry have noticed that they can't bound up a flight of stairs like they used to, without their heart fluttering a little.

All that can happen in a thousand days.

Nature's been pushing and contriving in other ways, too: a number of young people fell in love and got married.

Yes, the mountain got bit away a few fractions of an inch; millions of gallons of water went by the mill; and here and there a new home was set up under a roof.

Almost everybody in the world gets married,—you know what I mean? In our town there aren't hardly any exceptions. Most everybody in the world climbs into their graves married.

The First Act was called the Daily Life. This act is called Love and Marriage. There's another act coming after this: I reckon you can guess what that's about.

So:

It's three years later. It's 1904.

It's July 7th, just after High School Commencement.

That's the time most of our young people jump up and get married.

Soon as they've passed their last examinations in solid geometry and Cicero's Orations, looks like they suddenly feel themselves fit to be married.

It's early morning. Only this time it's been raining. It's been pouring and thundering.

Mrs. Gibbs' garden, and Mrs. Webb's here: drenched.

All those bean poles and pea vines: drenched.

All yesterday over there on Main Street, the rain looked like curtains being blown along.

Hm . . . it may begin again any minute.

There! You can hear the 5:45 for Boston.

> MRS. GIBBS *and* MRS. WEBB *enter their kitchen and start the day as in the First Act.*

And there's Mrs. Gibbs and Mrs. Webb come down to make breakfast, just as though it were an ordinary day. I don't have to point out to the women in my audience that those ladies they see before them, both of those ladies cooked three meals a day—one of 'em for twenty years, the other for forty—and no summer vacation. They brought up two children apiece, washed, cleaned the house,—and *never a nervous breakdown.*

It's like what one of those Middle West poets said: You've got to love life to have life, and you've got to have life to love life. . . . It's what they call a vicious circle.

HOWIE NEWSOME:

> *Off stage left.*

Giddap, Bessie!

STAGE MANAGER:

Here comes Howie Newsome delivering the milk. And there's Si Crowell delivering the papers like his brother before him.

> SI CROWELL *has entered hurling imaginary newspapers into doorways;* HOWIE NEWSOME *has come along Main Street with Bessie.*

SI CROWELL:

Morning, Howie.

HOWIE NEWSOME:

Morning, Si.—Anything in the papers I ought to know?

SI CROWELL:

Nothing much, except we're losing about the best baseball pitcher Grover's Corners ever had—George Gibbs.

HOWIE NEWSOME:

Reckon he is.

SI CROWELL:

He could hit and run bases, too.

HOWIE NEWSOME:

Yep. Mighty fine ball player.—Whoa! Bessie! I guess I can stop and talk if I've a mind to!

SI CROWELL:

I don't see how he could give up a thing like that just to get married. Would you, Howie?

HOWIE NEWSOME:

Can't tell, Si. Never had no talent that way.

> CONSTABLE WARREN *enters. They exchange good mornings.*
You're up early, Bill.

CONSTABLE WARREN:

Seein' if there's anything I can do to prevent a flood. River's been risin' all night.

HOWIE NEWSOME:

Si Crowell's all worked up here about George Gibbs' retiring from baseball.

CONSTABLE WARREN:

Yes, sir; that's the way it goes. Back in '84 we had a player, Si— even George Gibbs couldn't touch him. Name of Hank Todd. Went down to Maine and become a parson. Wonderful ball player.—Howie, how does the weather look to you?

HOWIE NEWSOME:

Oh, 'tain't bad. Think maybe it'll clear up for good.

> CONSTABLE WARREN *and* SI CROWELL *continue on their way.*
>
> HOWIE NEWSOME *brings the milk first to Mrs. Gibbs' house. She meets him by the trellis.*

MRS. GIBBS:

Good morning, Howie. Do you think it's going to rain again?

HOWIE NEWSOME:

Morning, Mrs. Gibbs. It rained so heavy, I think maybe it'll clear up.

MRS. GIBBS:

Certainly hope it will.

HOWIE NEWSOME:

How much did you want today?

MRS. GIBBS:

I'm going to have a houseful of relations, Howie. Looks to me like I'll need three-a-milk and two-a-cream.

HOWIE NEWSOME:

My wife says to tell you we both hope they'll be very happy, Mrs. Gibbs. Know they *will*.

MRS. GIBBS:

Thanks a lot, Howie. Tell your wife I hope she gits there to the wedding.

HOWIE NEWSOME:

Yes, she'll be there; she'll be there if she kin.
       HOWIE NEWSOME *crosses to Mrs. Webb's house.*
Morning, Mrs. Webb.

MRS. WEBB:

Oh, good morning, Mr. Newsome. I told you four quarts of milk, but I hope you can spare me another.

HOWIE NEWSOME:

Yes'm . . . and the two of cream.

MRS. WEBB:

Will it start raining again, Mr. Newsome?

HOWIE NEWSOME:

Well. Just sayin' to Mrs. Gibbs as how it may lighten up. Mrs. Newsome told me to tell you as how we hope they'll both be very happy, Mrs. Webb. Know they *will*.

MRS. WEBB:

Thank you, and thank Mrs. Newsome and we're counting on seeing you at the wedding.

HOWIE NEWSOME:

Yes, Mrs. Webb. We hope to git there. Couldn't miss that. Come on, Bessie.

> *Exit* HOWIE NEWSOME.
>
> DR. GIBBS *descends in shirt sleeves, and sits down at his breakfast table.*

DR. GIBBS:

Well, Ma, the day has come. You're losin' one of your chicks.

MRS. GIBBS:

Frank Gibbs, don't you say another word. I feel like crying every minute. Sit down and drink your coffee.

DR. GIBBS:

The groom's up shaving himself—only there ain't an awful lot to shave. Whistling and singing, like he's glad to leave us.—Every now and then he says "I do" to the mirror, but it don't sound convincing to me.

MRS. GIBBS:

I declare, Frank, I don't know how he'll get along. I've arranged his clothes and seen to it he's put warm things on,—Frank! they're too *young*. Emily won't think of such things. He'll catch his death of cold within a week.

DR. GIBBS:

I was remembering my wedding morning, Julia.

MRS. GIBBS:

Now don't start that, Frank Gibbs.

DR. GIBBS:

I was the scaredest young fella in the State of New Hampshire. I thought I'd make a mistake for sure. And when I saw you comin' down that aisle I thought you were the prettiest girl I'd ever seen, but the only trouble was that I'd never seen you before. There I was in the Congregational Church marryin' a total stranger.

MRS. GIBBS:

And how do you think I felt!—Frank, weddings are perfectly awful things. Farces,—that's what they are!
> *She puts a plate before him.*
Here, I've made something for you.

DR. GIBBS:

Why, Julia Hersey—French toast!

MRS. GIBBS:

'Tain't hard to make and I had to do *some*thing.
> *Pause.* DR. GIBBS *pours on the syrup.*

DR. GIBBS:

How'd you sleep last night, Julia?

MRS. GIBBS:

Well, I heard a lot of the hours struck off.

DR. GIBBS:

Ye-e-s! I get a shock every time I think of George setting out to be a family man—that great gangling thing!—I tell you Julia, there's nothing so terrifying in the world as a *son*. The relation of father and son is the darndest, awkwardest—

MRS. GIBBS:

Well, mother and daughter's no picnic, let me tell you.

DR. GIBBS:

They'll have a lot of troubles, I suppose, but that's none of our business. Everybody has a right to their own troubles.

MRS. GIBBS:

> *At the table, drinking her coffee, meditatively.*

Yes . . . people are meant to go through life two by two. 'Tain't natural to be lonesome.

> *Pause.* DR. GIBBS *starts laughing.*

DR. GIBBS:

Julia, do you know one of the things I was scared of when I married you?

MRS. GIBBS:

Oh, go along with you!

DR. GIBBS:

I was afraid we wouldn't have material for conversation more'n'd last us a few weeks.

> *Both laugh.*

I was afraid we'd run out and eat our meals in silence, that's a fact.—Well, you and I been conversing for twenty years now without any noticeable barren spells.

MRS. GIBBS:

Well,—good weather, bad weather—'tain't very choice, but I always find something to say.

> *She goes to the foot of the stairs.*

Did you hear Rebecca stirring around upstairs?

DR. GIBBS:

No. Only day of the year Rebecca hasn't been managing everybody's business up there. She's hiding in her room.—I got the impression she's crying.

MRS. GIBBS:

Lord's sakes!—This has got to stop.—Rebecca! Rebecca! Come and get your breakfast.

> GEORGE *comes rattling down the stairs, very brisk.*

GEORGE:

Good morning, everybody. Only five more hours to live.

> *Makes the gesture of cutting his throat, and a loud "k-k-k," and starts through the trellis.*

MRS. GIBBS:

George Gibbs, where are you going?

GEORGE:

Just stepping across the grass to see my girl.

MRS. GIBBS:

Now, George! You put on your overshoes. It's raining torrents. You don't go out of this house without you're prepared for it.

GEORGE:

Aw, Ma. It's just a *step!*

MRS. GIBBS:

George! You'll catch your death of cold and cough all through the service.

DR. GIBBS:

George, do as your mother tells you!

> DR. GIBBS *goes upstairs.*
>
> GEORGE *returns reluctantly to the kitchen and pantomimes putting on overshoes.*

MRS. GIBBS:

From tomorrow on you can kill yourself in all weathers, but while you're in my house you'll live wisely, thank you.—Maybe

Mrs. Webb isn't used to callers at seven in the morning.—Here, take a cup of coffee first.

GEORGE:

Be back in a minute.

He crosses the stage, leaping over the puddles.

Good morning, Mother Webb.

MRS. WEBB:

Goodness! You frightened me!—Now, George, you can come in a minute out of the wet, but you know I can't ask you in.

GEORGE:

Why not—?

MRS. WEBB:

George, you know's well as I do: the groom can't see his bride on his wedding day, not until he sees her in church.

GEORGE:

Aw!—that's just a superstition.—Good morning, Mr. Webb.

Enter MR. WEBB.

MR. WEBB:

Good morning, George.

GEORGE:

Mr. Webb, you don't believe in that superstition, do you?

MR. WEBB:

There's a lot of common sense in some superstitions, George.

He sits at the table, facing right.

MRS. WEBB:

Millions have folla'd it, George, and you don't want to be the first to fly in the face of custom.

GEORGE:

How is Emily?

MRS. WEBB:

She hasn't waked up yet. I haven't heard a sound out of her.

GEORGE:

Emily's *asleep*!!!

MRS. WEBB:

No wonder! We were up 'til all hours, sewing and packing. Now I'll tell you what I'll do; you set down here a minute with Mr. Webb and drink this cup of coffee; and I'll go upstairs and see she doesn't come down and surprise you. There's some bacon, too; but don't be long about it.

> *Exit* MRS. WEBB.
> *Embarrassed silence.*
> MR. WEBB *dunks doughnuts in his coffee.*
> *More silence.*

MR. WEBB:

> *Suddenly and loudly.*

Well, George, how are you?

GEORGE:

> *Startled, choking over his coffee.*

Oh, fine, I'm fine.

> *Pause.*

Mr. Webb, what sense could there be in a superstition like that?

MR. WEBB:

Well, you see,—on her wedding morning a girl's head's apt to be full of . . . clothes and one thing and another. Don't you think that's probably it?

GEORGE:

Ye-e-s. I never thought of that.

MR. WEBB:

A girl's apt to be a mite nervous on her wedding day.
> *Pause.*

GEORGE:

I wish a fellow could get married without all that marching up and down.

MR. WEBB:

Every man that's ever lived has felt that way about it, George; but it hasn't been any use. It's the womenfolk who've built up weddings, my boy. For a while now the women have it all their own. A man looks pretty small at a wedding, George. All those good women standing shoulder to shoulder making sure that the knot's tied in a mighty public way.

GEORGE:

But . . . you *believe* in it, don't you, Mr. Webb?

MR. WEBB:

> *With alacrity.*

Oh, yes; *oh, yes.* Don't you misunderstand me, my boy. Marriage is a wonderful thing,—wonderful thing. And don't you forget that, George.

GEORGE:

No, sir.—Mr. Webb, how old were you when you got married?

MR. WEBB:

Well, you see: I'd been to college and I'd taken a little time to get settled. But Mrs. Webb—she wasn't much older than what

Emily is. Oh, age hasn't much to do with it, George,—not compared with . . . uh . . . other things.

GEORGE:

What were you going to say, Mr. Webb?

MR. WEBB:

Oh, I don't know.—Was I going to say something?
Pause.
George, I was thinking the other night of some advice my father gave me when I got married. Charles, he said, Charles, start out early showing who's boss, he said. Best thing to do is to give an order, even if it don't make sense; just so she'll learn to obey. And he said: if anything about your wife irritates you—her conversation, or anything—just get up and leave the house. That'll make it clear to her, he said. And, oh, yes! he said never, *never* let your wife know how much money you have, never.

GEORGE:

Well, Mr. Webb . . . I don't think I could . . .

MR. WEBB:

So I took the opposite of my father's advice and I've been happy ever since. And let that be a lesson to you, George, never to ask advice on personal matters.—George, are you going to raise chickens on your farm?

GEORGE:

What?

MR. WEBB:

Are you going to raise chickens on your farm?

GEORGE:

Uncle Luke's never been much interested, but I thought—

MR. WEBB:

A book came into my office the other day, George, on the Philo System of raising chickens. I want you to read it. I'm thinking of beginning in a small way in the back yard, and I'm going to put an incubator in the cellar—

> *Enter* MRS. WEBB.

MRS. WEBB:

Charles, are you talking about that old incubator again? I thought you two'd be talking about things worth while.

MR. WEBB:

> *Bitingly.*

Well, Myrtle, if you want to give the boy some good advice, I'll go upstairs and leave you alone with him.

MRS. WEBB:

> *Pulling* GEORGE *up.*

George, Emily's got to come downstairs and eat her breakfast. She sends you her love but she doesn't want to lay eyes on you. Good-by.

GEORGE:

Good-by.

> GEORGE *crosses the stage to his own home, bewildered and crestfallen. He slowly dodges a puddle and disappears into his house.*

MR. WEBB:

Myrtle, I guess you don't know about that older superstition.

MRS. WEBB:

What do you mean, Charles?

MR. WEBB:

Since the cave men: no bridegroom should see his father-in-law on the day of the wedding, or near it. Now remember that.

Both leave the stage.

STAGE MANAGER:

Thank you very much, Mr. and Mrs. Webb.—Now I have to interrupt again here. You see, we want to know how all this began —this wedding, this plan to spend a lifetime together. I'm awfully interested in how big things like that begin.

You know how it is: you're twenty-one or twenty-two and you make some decisions; then whisss! you're seventy: you've been a lawyer for fifty years, and that white-haired lady at your side has eaten over fifty thousand meals with you.

How do such things begin?

George and Emily are going to show you now the conversation they had when they first knew that . . . that . . . as the saying goes . . . they were meant for one another.

But before they do it I want you to try and remember what it was like to have been very young.

And particularly the days when you were first in love; when you were like a person sleepwalking, and you didn't quite see the street you were in, and didn't quite hear everything that was said to you.

You're just a little bit crazy. Will you remember that, please?

Now they'll be coming out of high school at three o'clock. George has just been elected President of the Junior Class, and as it's June, that means he'll be President of the Senior Class all next year. And Emily's just been elected Secretary and Treasurer. I don't have to tell you how important that is.

He places a board across the backs of two chairs, which he takes from those at the Gibbs family's table. He brings

ACT TWO

*two high stools from the wings and places them behind
the board. Persons sitting on the stools will be facing the
audience. This is the counter of Mr. Morgan's drugstore.
The sounds of young people's voices are heard off left.*

Yepp,—there they are coming down Main Street now.

*EMILY, carrying an armful of—imaginary—schoolbooks,
comes along Main Street from the left.*

EMILY:

I can't, Louise. I've got to go home. Good-by. Oh, Ernestine!
Ernestine! Can you come over tonight and do Latin? Isn't that
Cicero the worst thing—! Tell your mother you *have* to. G'by.
G'by, Helen. G'by, Fred.

GEORGE, also carrying books, catches up with her.

GEORGE:

Can I carry your books home for you, Emily?

EMILY:

> *Coolly.*

Why . . . uh . . . Thank you. It isn't far.

> *She gives them to him.*

GEORGE:

Excuse me a minute, Emily.—Say, Bob, if I'm a little late, start
practice anyway. And give Herb some long high ones.

EMILY:

Good-by, Lizzy.

GEORGE:

Good-by, Lizzy.—I'm awfully glad you were elected, too, Emily.

EMILY:

Thank you.

> *They have been standing on Main Street, almost against*

the back wall. They take the first steps toward th
audience when GEORGE *stops and says:*

GEORGE:

Emily, why are you mad at me?

EMILY:

I'm not mad at you.

GEORGE:

You've been treating me so funny lately.

EMILY:

Well, since you ask me, I might as well say it right out, George,—
She catches sight of a teacher passing.
Good-by, Miss Corcoran.

GEORGE:

Good-by, Miss Corcoran.—Wha—what is it?

EMILY:

Not scoldingly; finding it difficult to say.
I don't like the whole change that's come over you in the last year
I'm sorry if that hurts your feelings, but I've got to—tell the truth
and shame the devil.

GEORGE:

A *change*?—Wha—what do you mean?

EMILY:

Well, up to a year ago I used to like you a lot. And I used
to watch you as you did everything . . . because we'd been friend
so long . . . and then you began spending all your time at *baseba*
. . . and you never stopped to speak to anybody any more. No
even to your own family you didn't . . . and, George, it's a fact

you've got awful conceited and stuck-up, and all the girls say so. They may not say so to your face, but that's what they say about you behind your back, and it hurts me to hear them say it, but I've got to agree with them a little. I'm sorry if it hurts your feelings . . . but I can't be sorry I said it.

GEORGE:

I . . . I'm glad you said it, Emily. I never thought that such a thing was happening to me. I guess it's hard for a fella not to have faults creep into his character.

> *They take a step or two in silence, then stand still in misery.*

EMILY:

I always expect a man to be perfect and I think he should be.

GEORGE:

Oh . . . I don't think it's possible to be perfect, Emily.

EMILY:

Well, my *father* is, and as far as I can see *your* father is. There's no reason on earth why you shouldn't be, too.

GEORGE:

Well, I feel it's the other way round. That men aren't naturally good; but girls are.

EMILY:

Well, you might as well know right now that I'm not perfect. It's not as easy for a girl to be perfect as a man, because we girls are more—more—nervous.—Now I'm sorry I said all that about you. I don't know what made me say it.

GEORGE:

Emily,—

EMILY:

Now I can see it's not the truth at all. And I suddenly feel that it isn't important, anyway.

GEORGE:

Emily . . . would you like an ice-cream soda, or something, before you go home?

EMILY:

Well, thank you. . . . I would.

> *They advance toward the audience and make an abrupt right turn, opening the door of Morgan's drugstore. Under strong emotion, EMILY keeps her face down. GEORGE speaks to some passers-by.*

GEORGE:

Hello, Stew,—how are you?—Good afternoon, Mrs. Slocum.

> *The STAGE MANAGER, wearing spectacles and assuming the role of Mr. Morgan, enters abruptly from the right and stands between the audience and the counter of his soda fountain.*

STAGE MANAGER:

Hello, George. Hello, Emily.—What'll you have?—Why, Emily Webb,—what you been crying about?

GEORGE:

> *He gropes for an explanation.*

She . . . she just got an awful scare, Mr. Morgan. She almost got run over by that hardware-store wagon. Everybody says that Tom Huckins drives like a crazy man.

STAGE MANAGER:

> *Drawing a drink of water.*

Well, now! You take a drink of water, Emily. You look all shook up. I tell you, you've got to look both ways before you cross Main Street these days. Gets worse every year.—What'll you have?

EMILY:

I'll have a strawberry phosphate, thank you, Mr. Morgan.

GEORGE:

No, no, Emily. Have an ice-cream soda with me. Two strawberry ice-cream sodas, Mr. Morgan.

STAGE MANAGER:

> *Working the faucets.*

Two strawberry ice-cream sodas, yes sir. Yes, sir. There are a hundred and twenty-five horses in Grover's Corners this minute I'm talking to you. State Inspector was in here yesterday. And now they're bringing in these auto-mo-biles, the best thing to do is to just stay home. Why, I can remember when a dog could go to sleep all day in the middle of Main Street and nothing come along to disturb him.

> *He sets the imaginary glasses before them.*

There they are. Enjoy 'em.

> *He sees a customer, right.*

Yes, Mrs. Ellis. What can I do for you?

> *He goes out right.*

EMILY:

They're so expensive.

GEORGE:

No, no,—don't you think of that. We're celebrating our election. And then do you know what else I'm celebrating?

EMILY:

N-no.

GEORGE:

I'm celebrating because I've got a friend who tells me all the things that ought to be told me.

EMILY:

George, *please* don't think of that. I don't know why I said it. It's not true. You're—

GEORGE:

No, Emily, you stick to it. I'm glad you spoke to me like you did. But you'll *see*: I'm going to change so quick—you bet I'm going to change. And, Emily, I want to ask you a favor.

EMILY:

What?

GEORGE:

Emily, if I go away to State Agriculture College next year, will you write me a letter once in a while?

EMILY:

I certainly will. I certainly will, George . . .
        Pause. They start sipping the sodas through the straws.
It certainly seems like being away three years you'd get out of touch with things. Maybe letters from Grover's Corners wouldn't be so interesting after a while. Grover's Corners isn't a very important place when you think of all—New Hampshire; but I think it's a very nice town.

GEORGE:

The day wouldn't come when I wouldn't want to know everything that's happening here. I know *that's* true, Emily.

EMILY:

Well, I'll try to make my letters interesting.
        Pause.

GEORGE:

Y'know. Emily, whenever I meet a farmer I ask him if he thinks it's important to go to Agriculture School to be a good farmer.

EMILY:

Why, George—

GEORGE:

Yeah, and some of them say that it's even a waste of time. You can get all those things, anyway, out of the pamphlets the government sends out. And Uncle Luke's getting old,—he's about ready for me to start in taking over his farm tomorrow, if I could.

EMILY:

My!

GEORGE:

And, like you say, being gone all that time . . . in other places and meeting other people . . . Gosh, if anything like that can happen I don't want to go away. I guess new people aren't any better than old ones. I'll bet they almost never are. Emily . . . I feel that you're as good a friend as I've got. I don't need to go and meet the people in other towns.

EMILY:

But, George, maybe it's very important for you to go and learn all that about—cattle judging and soils and those things. . . . Of course, I don't know.

GEORGE:

After a pause, very seriously.
Emily, I'm going to make up my mind right now. I won't go. I'll tell Pa about it tonight.

EMILY:

Why, George, I don't see why you have to decide right now. It's a whole year away.

GEORGE:

Emily, I'm glad you spoke to me about that . . . that fault in my character. What you said was right; but there was *one* thing wrong in it, and that was when you said that for a year I wasn't noticing people, and . . . you, for instance. Why, you say you were watching me when I did everything . . . I was doing the same about you all the time. Why, sure,—I always thought about you as one of the chief people I thought about. I always made sure where you were sitting on the bleachers, and who you were with, and for three days now I've been trying to walk home with you; but something's always got in the way. Yesterday I was standing over against the wall waiting for you, and you walked home with *Miss Corcoran*.

EMILY:

George! . . . Life's awful funny! How could I have known that? Why, I thought—

GEORGE:

Listen, Emily, I'm going to tell you why I'm not going to Agriculture School. I think that once you've found a person that you're very fond of . . . I mean a person who's fond of you, too, and likes you enough to be interested in your character . . . Well, I think that's just as important as college is, and even more so. That's what I think.

EMILY:

I think it's awfully important, too.

GEORGE:

Emily.

EMILY:

Y-yes, George.

GEORGE:

Emily, if I *do* improve and make a big change . . . would you be
. . . I mean: *could* you be . . .

EMILY:

I . . . I am now; I always have been.

GEORGE:

> *Pause.*

So I guess this is an important talk we've been having.

EMILY:

Yes . . . yes.

GEORGE:

> *Takes a deep breath and straightens his back.*

Wait just a minute and I'll walk you home.

> *With mounting alarm he digs into his pockets for the*
> *money.*
> *The* STAGE MANAGER *enters, right.*
> GEORGE, *deeply embarrassed, but direct, says to him:*

Mr. Morgan, I'll have to go home and get the money to pay you
for this. It'll only take me a minute.

STAGE MANAGER:

> *Pretending to be affronted.*

What's that? George Gibbs, do you mean to tell me—!

GEORGE:

Yes, but I had reasons, Mr. Morgan.—Look, here's my gold watch
to keep until I come back with the money.

STAGE MANAGER:

That's all right. Keep your watch. I'll trust you.

GEORGE:

I'll be back in five minutes.

STAGE MANAGER:

I'll trust you ten years, George,—not a day over.—Got all over your shock, Emily?

EMILY:

Yes, thank you, Mr. Morgan. It was nothing.

GEORGE:

Taking up the books from the counter.

I'm ready.

They walk in grave silence across the stage and pass through the trellis at the Webbs' back door and disappear.

The STAGE MANAGER watches them go out, then turns to the audience, removing his spectacles.

STAGE MANAGER:

Well,—

He claps his hands as a signal.

Now we're ready to get on with the wedding.

He stands waiting while the set is prepared for the next scene.

STAGEHANDS remove the chairs, tables and trellises from the Gibbs and Webb houses.

They arrange the pews for the church in the center of the stage. The congregation will sit facing the back wall. The aisle of the church starts at the center of the back wall and comes toward the audience.

ACT TWO

A small platform is placed against the back wall on which the STAGE MANAGER *will stand later, playing the minister. The image of a stained-glass window is cast from a lantern slide upon the back wall.*

When all is ready the STAGE MANAGER *strolls to the center of the stage, down front, and, musingly, addresses the audience.*

There are a lot of things to be said about a wedding; there are a lot of thoughts that go on during a wedding.

We can't get them all into one wedding, naturally, and especially not into a wedding at Grover's Corners, where they're awfully plain and short.

In this wedding I play the minister. That gives me the right to say a few more things about it.

For a while now, the play gets pretty serious.

Y'see, some churches say that marriage is a sacrament. I don't quite know what that means, but I can guess. Like Mrs. Gibbs said a few minutes ago: People were made to live two-by-two.

This is a good wedding, but people are so put together that even at a good wedding there's a lot of confusion way down deep in people's minds and we thought that that ought to be in our play, too.

The real hero of this scene isn't on the stage at all, and you know who that is. It's like what one of those European fellas said: every child born into the world is nature's attempt to make a perfect human being. Well, we've seen nature pushing and contriving for some time now. We all know that nature's interested in quantity; but I think she's interested in quality, too,—that's why I'm in the ministry.

And don't forget all the other witnesses at this wedding,—the ancestors. Millions of them. Most of them set out to live two-by-two, also. Millions of them.

Well, that's all my sermon. 'Twan't very long, anyway.

The organ starts playing Handel's "Largo."

The congregation streams into the church and sits in silence.

Church bells are heard.

MRS. GIBBS *sits in the front row, the first seat on the aisle, the right section; next to her are* REBECCA *and* DR. GIBBS. *Across the aisle* MRS. WEBB, WALLY *and* MR. WEBB. *A small choir takes its place, facing the audience under the stained-glass window.*

MRS. WEBB, *on the way to her place, turns back and speaks to the audience.*

MRS. WEBB:

I don't know why on earth I should be crying. I suppose there's nothing to cry about. It came over me at breakfast this morning; there was Emily eating her breakfast as she's done for seventeen years and now she's going off to eat it in someone else's house. I suppose that's it.

And Emily! She suddenly said: I can't eat another mouthful, and she put her head down on the table and *she* cried.

She starts toward her seat in the church, but turns back and adds:

Oh, I've got to say it: you know, there's something downright cruel about sending our girls out into marriage this way.

I hope some of her girl friends have told her a thing or two. It's cruel, I know, but I couldn't bring myself to say anything. I went into it blind as a bat myself.

In half-amused exasperation.

The whole world's wrong, that's what's the matter.

There they come.

She hurries to her place in the pew.

GEORGE *starts to come down the right aisle of the theatre,
through the audience.*

Suddenly THREE MEMBERS *of his baseball team appear by
the right proscenium pillar and start whistling and catcall-
ing to him. They are dressed for the ball field.*

THE BASEBALL PLAYERS:

Eh, George, George! Hast—yaow! Look at him, fellas—he looks
scared to death. Yaow! George, don't look so innocent, you old
geezer. We know what you're thinking. Don't disgrace the team,
big boy. Whoo-oo-oo.

STAGE MANAGER:

All right! All right! That'll do. That's enough of that.

> *Smiling, he pushes them off the stage. They lean back to
> shout a few more catcalls.*

There used to be an awful lot of that kind of thing at weddings
in the old days,—Rome, and later. We're more civilized now,—
so they say.

> *The choir starts singing "Love Divine, All Love Ex-
> celling—."* GEORGE *has reached the stage. He stares at the
> congregation a moment, then takes a few steps of with-
> drawal, toward the right proscenium pillar. His mother,
> from the front row, seems to have felt his confusion. She
> leaves her seat and comes down the aisle quickly to him.*

MRS. GIBBS:

George! George! What's the matter?

GEORGE:

Ma, I don't want to grow old. Why's everybody pushing me so?

MRS. GIBBS:

Why, George . . . you wanted it.

GEORGE:

No, Ma, listen to me—

MRS. GIBBS:

No, no, George,—you're a man now.

GEORGE:

Listen, Ma,—for the last time I ask you . . . All I want to do is to be a fella—

MRS. GIBBS:

George! If anyone should hear you! Now stop. Why, I'm ashamed of you!

GEORGE:

> *He comes to himself and looks over the scene.*

What? Where's Emily?

MRS. GIBBS:

> *Relieved.*

George! You gave me such a turn.

GEORGE:

Cheer up, Ma. I'm getting married.

MRS. GIBBS:

Let me catch my breath a minute.

GEORGE:

> *Comforting her.*

Now, Ma, you save Thursday nights. Emily and I are coming over to dinner every Thursday night . . . you'll see. Ma, what are you crying for? Come on; we've got to get ready for this.

> MRS. GIBBS, *mastering her emotion, fixes his tie and whispers to him.*

In the meantime, EMILY, *in white and wearing her wedding veil, has come through the audience and mounted onto the stage. She too draws back, frightened, when she sees the congregation in the church. The choir begins: "Blessed Be the Tie That Binds."*

EMILY:

I never felt so alone in my whole life. And George over there, looking so . . .! I *hate* him. I wish I were dead. Papa! Papa!

MR. WEBB:

Leaves his seat in the pews and comes toward her anxiously.

Emily! Emily! Now don't get upset. . . .

EMILY:

But, Papa,—I don't want to get married. . . .

MR. WEBB:

Sh—sh—Emily. Everything's all right.

EMILY:

Why can't I stay for a while just as I am? Let's go away,—

MR. WEBB:

No, no, Emily. Now stop and think a minute.

EMILY:

Don't you remember that you used to say,—all the time you used to say—all the time: that I was *your* girl! There must be lots of places we can go to. I'll work for you. I could keep house.

MR. WEBB:

Sh . . . You mustn't think of such things. You're just nervous, Emily.

He turns and calls:

George! George! Will you come here a minute?

He leads her toward George.

Why you're marrying the best young fellow in the world. George is a fine fellow.

EMILY:

But Papa,—

MRS. GIBBS returns unobtrusively to her seat.

MR. WEBB has one arm around his daughter. He places his hand on GEORGE's shoulder.

MR. WEBB:

I'm giving away my daughter, George. Do you think you can take care of her?

GEORGE:

Mr. Webb, I want to . . . I want to try. Emily, I'm going to do my best. I love you, Emily. I need you.

EMILY:

Well, if you love me, help me. All I want is someone to love me.

GEORGE:

I will, Emily. Emily, I'll try.

EMILY:

And I mean for *ever*. Do you hear? For ever and ever.

They fall into each other's arms.

The March from Lohengrin *is heard.*

The STAGE MANAGER, as CLERGYMAN, stands on the box, up center.

MR. WEBB:

Come, they're waiting for us. Now you know it'll be all right. Come, quick.

> GEORGE *slips away and takes his place beside the* STAGE
> MANAGER-CLERGYMAN.
> EMILY *proceeds up the aisle on her father's arm.*

STAGE MANAGER:

Do you, George, take this woman, Emily, to be your wedded wife,
to have . . .

> MRS. SOAMES *has been sitting in the last row of the congre-*
> *gation.*
> *She now turns to her neighbors and speaks in a shrill voice.*
> *Her chatter drowns out the rest of the clergyman's words.*

MRS. SOAMES:

Perfectly lovely wedding! Loveliest wedding I ever saw. Oh, I
do love a good wedding, don't you? Doesn't she make a lovely
bride?

GEORGE:

I do.

STAGE MANAGER:

Do you, Emily, take this man, George, to be your wedded
husband,—

> *Again his further words are covered by those of* MRS.
> SOAMES.

MRS. SOAMES:

Don't know *when* I've seen such a lovely wedding. But I always
cry. Don't know why it is, but I always cry. I just like to see
young people happy, don't you? Oh, I think it's lovely.

> *The ring.*
> *The kiss.*
> *The stage is suddenly arrested into silent tableau.*
> *The* STAGE MANAGER, *his eyes on the distance, as though*
> *to himself:*

77

OUR TOWN

STAGE MANAGER:

I've married over two hundred couples in my day.

Do I believe in it?

I don't know.

M.... marries N.... millions of them.

The cottage, the go-cart, the Sunday-afternoon drives in the Ford, the first rheumatism, the grandchildren, the second rheumatism, the deathbed, the reading of the will,—

> *He now looks at the audience for the first time, with a warm smile that removes any sense of cynicism from the next line.*

Once in a thousand times it's interesting.

—Well, let's have Mendelssohn's "Wedding March"!

> *The organ picks up the March.*
>
> *The* BRIDE *and* GROOM *come down the aisle, radiant, but trying to be very dignified.*

MRS. SOAMES:

Aren't they a lovely couple? Oh, I've never been to such a nice wedding. I'm sure they'll be happy. I always say: *happiness,* that's the great thing! The important thing is to be happy.

> *The* BRIDE *and* GROOM *reach the steps leading into the audience. A bright light is thrown upon them. They descend into the auditorium and run up the aisle joyously.*

STAGE MANAGER:

That's all the Second Act, folks. Ten minutes' intermission.

CURTAIN

ACT III

During the intermission the audience has seen the STAGE-HANDS arranging the stage. On the right-hand side, a little right of the center, ten or twelve ordinary chairs have been placed in three openly spaced rows facing the audience.

These are graves in the cemetery.

Toward the end of the intermission the ACTORS enter and take their places. The front row contains: toward the center of the stage, an empty chair; then MRS. GIBBS; SIMON STIMSON.

The second row contains, among others, MRS. SOAMES. The third row has WALLY WEBB.

The dead do not turn their heads or their eyes to right or left, but they sit in a quiet without stiffness. When they speak their tone is matter-of-fact, without sentimentality and, above all, without lugubriousness.

The STAGE MANAGER takes his accustomed place and waits for the house lights to go down.

STAGE MANAGER:

This time nine years have gone by, friends—summer, 1913.

Gradual changes in Grover's Corners. Horses are getting rarer. Farmers coming into town in Fords.

Everybody locks their house doors now at night. Ain't been any burglars in town yet, but everybody's heard about 'em.

You'd be surprised, though—on the whole, things don't change much around here.

This is certainly an important part of Grover's Corners. It's on a hilltop—a windy hilltop—lots of sky, lots of clouds,—often lots of sun and moon and stars.

You come up here, on a fine afternoon and you can see range on range of hills—awful blue they are—up there by Lake Sunapee and Lake Winnipesaukee . . . and way up, if you've got a glass, you can see the White Mountains and Mt. Washington—where North Conway and Conway is. And, of course, our favorite mountain, Mt. Monadnock, 's right here—and all these towns that lie around it: Jaffrey, 'n East Jaffrey, 'n Peterborough, 'n Dublin; and

> *Then pointing down in the audience.*

there, quite a ways down, is Grover's Corners.

Yes, beautiful spot up here. Mountain laurel and li-lacks. I often wonder why people like to be buried in Woodlawn and Brooklyn when they might pass the same time up here in New Hampshire. Over there—

> *Pointing to stage left.*

are the old stones,—1670, 1680. Strong-minded people that come a long way to be independent. Summer people walk around there laughing at the funny words on the tombstones . . . it don't do any harm. And genealogists come up from Boston—get paid by city people for looking up their ancestors. They want to make sure they're Daughters of the American Revolution and of the *Mayflower*. . . . Well, I guess that don't do any harm, either. Wherever you come near the human race, there's layers and layers of nonsense. . . .

Over there are some Civil War veterans. Iron flags on their graves . . . New Hampshire boys . . . had a notion that the Union ought to be kept together, though they'd never seen more than fifty miles of it themselves. All they knew was the name, friends—the United States of America. The United States of America. And they went and died about it.

This here is the new part of the cemetery. Here's your friend Mrs. Gibbs. 'N let me see—Here's Mr. Stimson, organist at the Congregational Church. And Mrs. Soames who enjoyed the wedding so—you remember? Oh, and a lot of others. And Editor Webb's boy, Wallace, whose appendix burst while he was on a Boy Scout trip to Crawford Notch.

Yes, an awful lot of sorrow has sort of quieted down up here. People just wild with grief have brought their relatives up to this hill. We all know how it is . . . and then time . . . and sunny days . . . and rainy days . . . 'n snow . . . We're all glad they're in a beautiful place and we're coming up here ourselves when our fit's over.

Now there are some things we all know, but we don't take'm out and look at'm very often. We all know that *something* is eternal. And it ain't houses and it ain't names, and it ain't earth, and it ain't even the stars . . . everybody knows in their bones that *something* is eternal, and that something has to do with human beings. All the greatest people ever lived have been telling us that for five thousand years and yet you'd be surprised how people are always losing hold of it. There's something way down deep that's eternal about every human being.

> *Pause.*

You know as well as I do that the dead don't stay interested in us living people for very long. Gradually, gradually, they lose hold of the earth . . . and the ambitions they had . . . and the pleasures they had . . . and the things they suffered . . . and the people they loved.

They get weaned away from earth—that's the way I put it,—weaned away.

And they stay here while the earth part of 'em burns away, burns out; and all that time they slowly get indifferent to what's goin' on in Grover's Corners.

They're waitin'. They're waitin' for something that they feel is comin'. Something important, and great. Aren't they waitin' for the eternal part in them to come out clear?

Some of the things they're going to say maybe'll hurt your feelings—but that's the way it is: mother'n daughter . . . husband 'n wife . . . enemy 'n enemy . . . money 'n miser . . . all those terribly important things kind of grow pale around here. And what's left when memory's gone, and your identity, Mrs. Smith?

He looks at the audience a minute, then turns to the stage. Well! There are some *living* people. There's Joe Stoddard, our undertaker, supervising a new-made grave. And here comes a Grover's Corners boy, that left town to go out West.

JOE STODDARD *has hovered about in the background.* SAM CRAIG *enters left, wiping his forehead from the exertion. He carries an umbrella and strolls front.*

SAM CRAIG:

Good afternoon, Joe Stoddard.

JOE STODDARD:

Good afternoon, good afternoon. Let me see now: do I know you?

SAM CRAIG:

I'm Sam Craig.

JOE STODDARD:

Gracious sakes' alive! Of all people! I should'a knowed you'd be back for the funeral. You've been away a long time, Sam.

SAM CRAIG:

Yes, I've been away over twelve years. I'm in business out in Buffalo now, Joe. But I was in the East when I got news of my cousin's death, so I thought I'd combine things a little and come and see the old home. You look well.

JOE STODDARD:

Yes, yes, can't complain. Very sad, our journey today, Samuel.

SAM CRAIG:

Yes.

JOE STODDARD:

Yes, yes. I always say I hate to supervise when a young person is taken. They'll be here in a few minutes now. I had to come here early today—my son's supervisin' at the home.

SAM CRAIG:

Reading stones.

Old Farmer McCarty, I used to do chores for him—after school. He had the lumbago.

JOE STODDARD:

Yes, we brought Farmer McCarty here a number of years ago now.

SAM CRAIG:

Staring at Mrs. Gibbs' knees.

Why, this is my Aunt Julia . . . I'd forgotten that she'd . . . of course, of course.

JOE STODDARD:

Yes, Doc Gibbs lost his wife two-three years ago . . . about this time. And today's another pretty bad blow for him, too.

MRS. GIBBS:

To Simon Stimson: in an even voice.

That's my sister Carey's boy, Sam . . . Sam Craig.

SIMON STIMSON:

I'm always uncomfortable when *they're* around.

MRS. GIBBS:

Simon.

SAM CRAIG:

Do they choose their own verses much, Joe?

JOE STODDARD:

No . . . not usual. Mostly the bereaved pick a verse.

SAM CRAIG:

Doesn't sound like Aunt Julia. There aren't many of those Hersey sisters left now. Let me see: where are . . . I wanted to look at my father's and mother's . . .

JOE STODDARD:

Over there with the Craigs . . . Avenue F.

SAM CRAIG:

> *Reading Simon Stimson's epitaph.*

He was organist at church, wasn't he?—Hm, drank a lot, we used to say.

JOE STODDARD:

Nobody was supposed to know about it. He'd seen a peck of trouble.

> *Behind his hand.*

Took his own life, y' know?

SAM CRAIG:

Oh, did he?

JOE STODDARD:

Hung himself in the attic. They tried to hush it up, but of course it got around. He chose his own epy-taph. You can see it there. It ain't a verse exactly.

SAM CRAIG:

Why, it's just some notes of music—what is it?

JOE STODDARD:

Oh, I wouldn't know. It was wrote up in the Boston papers at the time.

SAM CRAIG:

Joe, what did she die of?

JOE STODDARD:

Who?

SAM CRAIG:

My cousin.

JOE STODDARD:

Oh, didn't you know? Had some trouble bringing a baby into the world. 'Twas her second, though. There's a little boy 'bout four years old.

SAM CRAIG:

> *Opening his umbrella.*

The grave's going to be over there?

JOE STODDARD:

Yes, there ain't much more room over here among the Gibbses, so they're opening up a whole new Gibbs section over by Avenue B. You'll excuse me now. I see they're comin'.

> *From left to center, at the back of the stage, comes a procession.* FOUR MEN *carry a casket, invisible to us. All the rest are under umbrellas. One can vaguely see:* DR. GIBBS,

GEORGE, *the* WEBBS, *etc. They gather about a grave in the back center of the stage, a little to the left of center.*

MRS. SOAMES:

Who is it, Julia?

MRS. GIBBS:

> *Without raising her eyes.*
My daughter-in-law, Emily Webb.

MRS. SOAMES:

> *A little surprised, but no emotion.*
Well, I declare! The road up here must have been awful muddy. What did she die of, Julia?

MRS. GIBBS:

In childbirth.

MRS. SOAMES:

Childbirth.

> *Almost with a laugh.*
I'd forgotten all about that. My, wasn't life awful—

> *With a sigh.*
and wonderful.

SIMON STIMSON:

> *With a sideways glance.*
Wonderful, was it?

MRS. GIBBS:

Simon! Now, remember!

MRS. SOAMES:

I remember Emily's wedding. Wasn't it a lovely wedding! And I remember her reading the class poem at Graduation Exercises.

Emily was one of the brightest girls ever graduated from High School. I've heard Principal Wilkins say so time after time. I called on them at their new farm, just before I died. Perfectly beautiful farm.

A WOMAN FROM AMONG THE DEAD:

It's on the same road we lived on.

A MAN AMONG THE DEAD:

Yepp, right smart farm.

> *They subside. The group by the grave starts singing "Blessed Be the Tie That Binds."*

A WOMAN AMONG THE DEAD:

I always liked that hymn. I was hopin' they'd sing a hymn.

> *Pause. Suddenly* EMILY *appears from among the umbrellas. She is wearing a white dress. Her hair is down her back and tied by a white ribbon like a little girl. She comes slowly, gazing wonderingly at the dead, a little dazed. She stops halfway and smiles faintly. After looking at the mourners for a moment, she walks slowly to the vacant chair beside Mrs. Gibbs and sits down.*

EMILY:

> *To them all, quietly, smiling.*

Hello.

MRS. SOAMES:

Hello, Emily.

A MAN AMONG THE DEAD:

Hello, M's Gibbs.

EMILY:

> *Warmly.*

Hello, Mother Gibbs.

MRS. GIBBS:

Emily.

EMILY:

Hello.

> *With surprise.*

It's raining.

> *Her eyes drift back to the funeral company.*

MRS. GIBBS:

Yes . . . They'll be gone soon, dear. Just rest yourself.

EMILY:

It seems thousands and thousands of years since I . . . Papa remembered that that was my favorite hymn.

Oh, I wish I'd been here a long time. I don't like being new here.—How do you do, Mr. Stimson?

SIMON STIMSON:

How do you do, Emily.

> EMILY *continues to look about her with a wondering smile; as though to shut out from her mind the thought of the funeral company she starts speaking to Mrs. Gibbs with a touch of nervousness.*

EMILY:

Mother Gibbs, George and I have made that farm into just the best place you ever saw. We thought of you all the time. We wanted to show you the new barn and a great long ce-ment drinking fountain for the stock. We bought that out of the money you left us.

MRS. GIBBS:

I did?

EMILY:

Don't you remember, Mother Gibbs—the legacy you left us? Why, it was over three hundred and fifty dollars.

MRS. GIBBS:

Yes, yes, Emily.

EMILY:

Well, there's a patent device on the drinking fountain so that it never overflows, Mother Gibbs, and it never sinks below a certain mark they have there. It's fine.

> *Her voice trails off and her eyes return to the funeral group.*

It won't be the same to George without me, but it's a lovely farm.

> *Suddenly she looks directly at Mrs. Gibbs.*

Live people don't understand, do they?

MRS. GIBBS:

No, dear—not very much.

EMILY:

They're sort of shut up in little boxes, aren't they? I feel as though I knew them last a thousand years ago . . . My boy is spending the day at Mrs. Carter's.

> *She sees* MR. CARTER *among the dead.*

Oh, Mr. Carter, my little boy is spending the day at your house.

MR. CARTER:

Is he?

EMILY:

Yes, he loves it there.—Mother Gibbs, we have a Ford, too. Never gives any trouble. I don't drive, though. Mother Gibbs, when does this feeling go away?—Of being . . . one of *them*? How long does it . . . ?

MRS. GIBBS:

Sh! dear. Just wait and be patient.

EMILY:

> *With a sigh.*

I know.—Look, they're finished. They're going.

MRS. GIBBS:

Sh—.

> *The umbrellas leave the stage.* DR. GIBBS *has come over to
> his wife's grave and stands before it a moment.* EMILY
> *looks up at his face.* MRS. GIBBS *does not raise her eyes.*

EMILY:

Look! Father Gibbs is bringing some of my flowers to you. He
looks just like George, doesn't he? Oh, Mother Gibbs, I never
realized before how troubled and how . . . how in the dark live
persons are. Look at him. I loved him so. From morning till night,
that's all they are—troubled.

> DR. GIBBS *goes off.*

THE DEAD:

Little cooler than it was.—Yes, that rain's cooled it off a little.
Those northeast winds always do the same thing, don't they?
If it isn't a rain, it's a three-day blow.—

> *A patient calm falls on the stage. The* STAGE MANAGER
> *appears at his proscenium pillar, smoking.* EMILY *sits up
> abruptly with an idea.*

EMILY:

But, Mother Gibbs, one can go back; one can go back there
again . . . into living. I feel it. I know it. Why just then for a
moment I was thinking about . . . about the farm . . . and for a
minute I *was* there, and my baby was on my lap as plain as day.

MRS. GIBBS:

Yes, of course you can.

EMILY:

I can go back there and live all those days over again . . . why not?

MRS. GIBBS:

All I can say is, Emily, don't.

EMILY:

> *She appeals urgently to the stage manager.*

But it's true, isn't it? I can go and live . . . back there . . . again.

STAGE MANAGER:

Yes, some have tried—but they soon come back here.

MRS. GIBBS:

Don't do it, Emily.

MRS. SOAMES:

Emily, don't. It's not what you think it'd be.

EMILY:

But I won't live over a sad day. I'll choose a happy one—I'll choose the day I first knew that I loved George. Why should that be painful?

> THEY *are silent. Her question turns to the stage manager.*

STAGE MANAGER:

You not only live it; but you watch yourself living it.

EMILY:

Yes?

STAGE MANAGER:

And as you watch it, you see the thing that they—down there—

never know. You see the future. You know what's going to happen afterwards.

EMILY:

But is that—painful? Why?

MRS. GIBBS:

That's not the only reason why you shouldn't do it, Emily. When you've been here longer you'll see that our life here is to forget all that, and think only of what's ahead, and be ready for what's ahead. When you've been here longer you'll understand.

EMILY:

Softly.
But, Mother Gibbs, how can I *ever* forget that life? It's all I know. It's all I had.

MRS. SOAMES:

Oh, Emily. It isn't wise. Really, it isn't.

EMILY:

But it's a thing I must know for myself. I'll choose a happy day, anyway.

MRS. GIBBS:

No!—At least, choose an unimportant day. Choose the least important day in your life. It will be important enough.

EMILY:

To herself.
Then it can't be since I was married; or since the baby was born.
To the stage manager, eagerly.
I can choose a birthday at least, can't I?—I choose my twelfth birthday.

ACT THREE

STAGE MANAGER:

All right. February 11th, 1899. A Tuesday.—Do you want any special time of day?

EMILY:

Oh, I want the whole day.

STAGE MANAGER:

We'll begin at dawn. You remember it had been snowing for several days; but it had stopped the night before, and they had begun clearing the roads. The sun's coming up.

EMILY:

> *With a cry; rising.*

There's Main Street . . . why, that's Mr. Morgan's drugstore before he changed it! . . . And there's the livery stable.

> *The stage at no time in this act has been very dark; but now the left half of the stage gradually becomes very bright—the brightness of a crisp winter morning.*
> EMILY *walks toward Main Street.*

STAGE MANAGER:

Yes, it's 1899. This is fourteen years ago.

EMILY:

Oh, that's the town I knew as a little girl. And, *look*, there's the old white fence that used to be around our house. Oh, I'd forgotten that! Oh, I love it so! Are they inside?

STAGE MANAGER:

Yes, your mother'll be coming downstairs in a minute to make breakfast.

EMILY:

> *Softly.*

Will she?

STAGE MANAGER:

And you remember: your father had been away for several day
he came back on the early-morning train.

EMILY:

No . . . ?

STAGE MANAGER:

He'd been back to his college to make a speech—in wester
New York, at Clinton.

EMILY:

Look! There's Howie Newsome. There's our policeman. B
he's *dead*; he *died.*

> The voices of HOWIE NEWSOME, CONSTABLE WARREN *an*
> JOE CROWELL, JR., *are heard at the left of the stage.* EMIL
> *listens in delight.*

HOWIE NEWSOME:

Whoa, Bessie!—Bessie! 'Morning, Bill.

CONSTABLE WARREN:

Morning, Howie.

HOWIE NEWSOME:

You're up early.

CONSTABLE WARREN:

Been rescuin' a party; darn near froze to death, down by Polis
Town thar. Got drunk and lay out in the snowdrifts. Thought h
was in bed when I shook'm.

EMILY:

Why, there's Joe Crowell. . . .

ACT THREE

JOE CROWELL:

Good morning, Mr. Warren. 'Morning, Howie.

> MRS. WEBB *has appeared in her kitchen, but* EMILY *does not see her until she calls.*

MRS. WEBB:

Chil-*dren!* Wally! Emily! . . . Time to get up.

EMILY:

Mama, I'm here! Oh! how young Mama looks! I didn't know Mama was ever that young.

MRS. WEBB:

You can come and dress by the kitchen fire, if you like; but hurry.

> HOWIE NEWSOME *has entered along Main Street and brings the milk to Mrs. Webb's door.*

Good morning, Mr. Newsome. Whhhh—it's cold.

HOWIE NEWSOME:

Ten below by my barn, Mrs. Webb.

MRS. WEBB:

Think of it! Keep yourself wrapped up.

> *She takes her bottles in, shuddering.*

EMILY:

> *With an effort.*

Mama, I can't find my blue hair ribbon anywhere.

MRS. WEBB:

Just open your eyes, dear, that's all. I laid it out for you special— on the dresser, there. If it were a snake it would bite you.

EMILY:

Yes, yes . . .

> *She puts her hand on her heart.* MR. WEBB *comes along*

95

Main Street, where he meets CONSTABLE WARREN. *Their movements and voices are increasingly lively in the sharp air.*

MR. WEBB:

Good morning, Bill.

CONSTABLE WARREN:

Good morning, Mr. Webb. You're up early.

MR. WEBB:

Yes, just been back to my old college in New York State. Been any trouble here?

CONSTABLE WARREN:

Well, I was called up this mornin' to rescue a Polish fella—darn near froze to death he was.

MR. WEBB:

We must get it in the paper.

CONSTABLE WARREN:

'Twan't much.

EMILY:

> *Whispers.*

Papa.

> MR. WEBB *shakes the snow off his feet and enters his house.*
> CONSTABLE WARREN *goes off, right.*

MR. WEBB:

Good morning, Mother.

MRS. WEBB:

How did it go, Charles?

MR. WEBB:

Oh, fine, I guess. I told'm a few things.—Everything all right here?

MRS. WEBB:

Yes—can't think of anything that's happened, special. Been right cold. Howie Newsome says it's ten below over to his barn.

MR. WEBB:

Yes, well, it's colder than that at Hamilton College. Students' ears are falling off. It ain't Christian.—Paper have any mistakes in it?

MRS. WEBB:

None that I noticed. Coffee's ready when you want it.

He starts upstairs.

Charles! Don't forget; it's Emily's birthday. Did you remember to get her something?

MR. WEBB:

Patting his pocket.

Yes, I've got something here.

Calling up the stairs.

Where's my girl? Where's my birthday girl?

He goes off left.

MRS. WEBB:

Don't interrupt her now, Charles. You can see her at breakfast. She's slow enough as it is. Hurry up, children! It's seven o'clock. Now, I don't want to call you again.

EMILY:

Softly, more in wonder than in grief.

I can't bear it. They're so young and beautiful. Why did they ever have to get old? Mama, I'm here. I'm grown up. I love you all, everything.—I can't look at everything hard enough.

She looks questioningly at the STAGE MANAGER, saying
suggesting: "Can I go in?" He nods briefly. She crosses
the inner door to the kitchen, left of her mother, and
though entering the room, says, suggesting the voice o
girl of twelve:

Good morning, Mama.

MRS. WEBB:

Crossing to embrace and kiss her; in her characteri
matter-of-fact manner.

Well, now, dear, a very happy birthday to my girl and ma
happy returns. There are some surprises waiting for you on
kitchen table.

EMILY:

Oh, Mama, you *shouldn't* have.
She throws an anguished glance at the stage manager.
I can't—I can't.

MRS. WEBB:

Facing the audience, over her stove.

But birthday or no birthday, I want you to eat your break
good and slow. I want you to grow up and be a good str
girl.
That in the blue paper is from your Aunt Carrie; and I reck
you can guess who brought the post-card album. I found it on
doorstep when I brought in the milk—George Gibbs . . . m
have come over in the cold pretty early . . . right nice of him

EMILY:

To herself.

Oh, George! I'd forgotten that. . . .

MRS. WEBB:

Chew that bacon good and slow. It'll help keep you warm on a cold day.

EMILY:

>   *With mounting urgency.*

Oh, Mama, just look at me one minute as though you really saw me. Mama, fourteen years have gone by. I'm dead. You're a grandmother, Mama. I married George Gibbs, Mama. Wally's dead, too. Mama, his appendix burst on a camping trip to North Conway. We felt just terrible about it—don't you remember? But, just for a moment now we're all together. Mama, just for a moment we're happy. *Let's look at one another.*

MRS. WEBB:

That in the yellow paper is something I found in the attic among your grandmother's things. You're old enough to wear it now, and I thought you'd like it.

EMILY:

And this is from you. Why, Mama, it's just lovely and it's just what I wanted. It's beautiful!

>   *She flings her arms around her mother's neck. Her*
>   MOTHER *goes on with her cooking, but is pleased.*

MRS. WEBB:

Well, I hoped you'd like it. Hunted all over. Your Aunt Norah couldn't find one in Concord, so I had to send all the way to Boston.

>   *Laughing.*

Wally has something for you, too. He made it at manual-training class and he's very proud of it. Be sure you make a big fuss about it.—Your father has a surprise for you, too; don't know what it is myself. Sh—here he comes.

MR. WEBB:

> *Off stage.*

Where's my girl? Where's my birthday girl?

EMILY:

> *In a loud voice to the stage manager.*

I can't. I can't go on. It goes so fast. We don't have time to look at one another.

> *She breaks down sobbing.*
>
> *The lights dim on the left half of the stage.* MRS. WEBB *disappears.*

I didn't realize. So all that was going on and we never noticed. Take me back—up the hill—to my grave. But first: Wait! One more look.

Good-by, Good-by, world. Good-by, Grover's Corners . . . Mama and Papa. Good-by to clocks ticking . . . and Mama's sunflowers. And food and coffee. And new-ironed dresses and hot baths . . . and sleeping and waking up. Oh, earth, you're too wonderful for anybody to realize you.

> *She looks toward the stage manager and asks abruptly, through her tears:*

Do any human beings ever realize life while they live it?—every, every minute?

STAGE MANAGER:

No.

> *Pause.*

The saints and poets, maybe—they do some.

EMILY:

I'm ready to go back.

> *She returns to her chair beside Mrs. Gibbs.*
> *Pause.*

MRS. GIBBS:

Were you happy?

EMILY:

No . . . I should have listened to you. That's all human beings are! Just blind people.

MRS. GIBBS:

Look, it's clearing up. The stars are coming out.

EMILY:

Oh, Mr. Stimson, I should have listened to them.

SIMON STIMSON:

> *With mounting violence; bitingly.*

Yes, now you know. Now you know! That's what it was to be alive. To move about in a cloud of ignorance; to go up and down trampling on the feelings of those . . . of those about you. To spend and waste time as though you had a million years. To be always at the mercy of one self-centered passion, or another. Now you know—that's the happy existence you wanted to go back to. Ignorance and blindness.

MRS. GIBBS:

> *Spiritedly.*

Simon Stimson, that ain't the whole truth and you know it. Emily, look at that star. I forget its name.

A MAN AMONG THE DEAD:

My boy Joel was a sailor,—knew 'em all. He'd set on the porch evenings and tell 'em all by name. Yes, sir, wonderful!

ANOTHER MAN AMONG THE DEAD:

A star's mighty good company.

A WOMAN AMONG THE DEAD:

Yes. Yes, 'tis.

SIMON STIMSON:

Here's one of *them* coming.

THE DEAD:

That's funny. 'Tain't no time for one of them to be here.—Goodness sakes.

EMILY:

Mother Gibbs, it's George.

MRS. GIBBS:

Sh, dear. Just rest yourself.

EMILY:

It's George.

> GEORGE *enters from the left, and slowly comes toward them.*

A MAN FROM AMONG THE DEAD:

And my boy, Joel, who knew the stars—he used to say it took millions of years for that speck o' light to git to the earth. Don't seem like a body could believe it, but that's what he used to say—millions of years.

> GEORGE *sinks to his knees then falls full length at Emily's feet.*

A WOMAN AMONG THE DEAD:

Goodness! That ain't no way to behave!

MRS. SOAMES:

He ought to be home.

EMILY:

Mother Gibbs?

MRS. GIBBS:

Yes, Emily?

EMILY:

They don't understand, do they?

MRS. GIBBS:

No, dear. They don't understand.

> *The* STAGE MANAGER *appears at the right, one hand on a dark curtain which he slowly draws across the scene.*
> *In the distance a clock is heard striking the hour very faintly.*

STAGE MANAGER:

Most everybody's asleep in Grover's Corners. There are a few lights on: Shorty Hawkins, down at the depot, has just watched the Albany train go by. And at the livery stable somebody's setting up late and talking.—Yes, it's clearing up. There are the stars—doing their old, old crisscross journeys in the sky. Scholars haven't settled the matter yet, but they seem to think there are no living beings up there. Just chalk . . . or fire. Only this one is straining away, straining away all the time to make something of itself. The strain's so bad that every sixteen hours everybody lies down and gets a rest.

> *He winds his watch.*

Hm. . . . Eleven o'clock in Grover's Corners.—You get a good rest, too. Good night.

THE END

Some Thoughts on Playwrighting*

By *Thornton Wilder*

Four fundamental conditions of the drama separate it from the other arts. Each of these conditions has its advantages and disadvantages, each requires a particular aptitude from the dramatist, and from each there are a number of instructive consequences to be derived. These conditions are:

1. The theater is an art which reposes upon the work of many collaborators;
2. It is addressed to the group-mind;
3. It is based upon a pretense and its very nature calls out a multiplication of pretenses;
4. Its action takes place in a perpetual present time.

1. THE THEATER IS AN ART WHICH REPOSES UPON THE WORK OF MANY COLLABORATORS.

We have been accustomed to think that a work of art is by definition the product of one governing selecting will.

A landscape by Cézanne consists of thousands of brush-strokes each commanded by one mind. *Paradise Lost* and *Pride and Prejudice*, even in cheap frayed copies, bear the immediate and exclusive message of one intelligence.

It is true that in musical performance we meet with

* From *Intent of the Artist*, edited by A. Centeno. Copyright 1941 by Princeton University Press.

intervening executants, but the element of intervention is slight compared to that which takes place in drama.

Illustrations:

1. One of the finest productions of *The Merchant of Venice* in our time showed Sir Henry Irving as Shylock, a noble, wronged and indignant being, of such stature that the Merchants of Venice dwindled before him into irresponsible schoolboys. He was confronted in court by a gracious, even queenly, Portia, Miss Ellen Terry. At the Odéon in Paris, however, Gémier played Shylock as a vengeful and hysterical buffoon, confronted in court by a Portia who was a *gamine* from the Paris streets with a lawyer's quill three feet long over her ear; at the close of the trial scene Shylock was driven screaming about the auditorium, behind the spectators' backs and onto the stage again, in a wild Elizabethan revel. Yet for all their divergences both were admirable productions of the play.

2. If there were ever a play in which fidelity to the author's requirements were essential in the representation of the principal rôle, it would seem to be Ibsen's *Hedda Gabler*, for the play is primarily an exposition of her character. Ibsen's directions read: "Enter from the left Hedda Gabler. She is a woman of twenty-nine. Her face and figure show great refinement and distinction Her complexion is pale and opaque. Her steel-gray eyes express an unruffled calm. Her hair is of an attractive medium brown, but is not particularly abundant; and she is dressed in a flowing loose-fitting morning gown." I once saw Eleonora Duse in this rôle. She was a woman of sixty and made no

effort to conceal it. Her complexion was pale and transparent. Her hair was white, and she was dressed in a gown that suggested some medieval empress in mourning. And the performance was very fine.

One may well ask: why write for the theater at all? Why not work in the novel where such deviations from one's intentions cannot take place?

There are two answers:

1. The theater presents certain vitalities of its own so inviting and stimulating that the writer is willing to receive them in compensation for this inevitable variation from an exact image.

2. The dramatist through working in the theater gradually learns not merely to take account of the presence of the collaborators, but to derive advantage from them; and he learns, above all, to organize the play in such a way that its strength lies not in appearances beyond his control, but in the succession of events and in the unfolding of an idea, in narration.

The gathered audience sits in a darkened room, one end of which is lighted. The nature of the transaction at which it is gazing is a succession of events illustrating a general idea—the stirring of the idea; the gradual feeding out of information; the shock and countershock of circumstances; the flow of action; the interruption of action; the moments of allusion to earlier events; the preparation of surprise, dread, or delight—all that is the author's and his alone.

For reasons to be discussed later—the expectancy of the group-mind, the problem of time on the stage, the absence of the narrator, the element of pretense—the theater carries the art of narration to a higher power than the novel or the epic poem. The theater is unfolding action and in the disposition of events the authors may exercise a governance so complete that the distortions effected by the physical appearance of actors, by the fancies of scene-painters and the misunderstandings of directors, fall into relative insignificance. It is just because the theater is an art of many collaborators, with the constant danger of grave misinterpretation, that the dramatist learns to turn his attention to the laws of narration, its logic and its deep necessity of presenting a unifying idea stronger than its mere collection of happenings. The dramatist must be by instinct a story teller.

There is something mysterious about the endowment of the story teller. Some very great writers possessed very little of it, and some others, lightly esteemed, possessed it in so large a measure that their books survive down the ages, to the confusion of severer critics. Alexandre Dumas had it to an extraordinary degree; while Melville, for all his splendid quality, had it barely sufficiently to raise his work from the realm of non-fiction. It springs, not, as some have said, from an aversion to general ideas, but from an instinctive coupling of idea and illustration; the idea, for a born story teller, can only be expressed imbedded in its circumstantial illustration. The myth, the parable, the fable are the fountainhead of all fiction and in them is seen most clearly the didactic, moralizing employment of a story. Modern taste shrinks from emphasizing the central idea that hides behind the fiction, but it exists there nevertheless, supplying the unity to fantasizing, and offering a justification to what otherwise we would repudiate as mere arbitrary contrivance, pretentious lying, or individualistic emotional association-spinning. For all their magnificent intellectual endowment, George Meredith and George Eliot were not born story tellers; they chose fiction as the vehicle for their reflections, and the passing of time is revealing their error in that choice. Jane Austen was pure story teller and her works are outlasting those of apparently more formidable rivals. The theater is more exacting than the novel in regard to this faculty and its presence constitutes a force which compensates the dramatist for the deviations which are introduced into his work by the presence of his collaborators.

The chief of these collaborators are the actors.

The actor's gift is a combination of three separate faculties or endowments. Their presence to a high degree in any one person is extremely rare, although the ambition to possess them is common. Those who rise to the height of the profession represent a selection and a struggle for survival in one of the most difficult and cruel of the artistic activities. The three endowments that compose the gift are observation, imagination and physical coordination.

1. An observant and analyzing eye for all modes of behavior about us, for dress and manner, and for the signs of thought and emotion in one's self and in others.

2. The strength of imagination and memory whereby the actor may, at the indication in the author's text, explore his store of observations and represent the details of appear-

ance and the intensity of the emotions—joy, fear, surprise, grief, love and hatred, and through imagination extend them to intenser degrees and to differing characterizations.

3. A physical coordination whereby the force of these inner realizations may be communicated to voice, face and body.

An actor must *know* the appearances and the mental states; he must *apply* his knowledge to the rôle; and he must physically *express* his knowledge. Moreover, his concentration must be so great that he can effect this representation under conditions of peculiar difficulty—in abrupt transition from the non-imaginative conditions behind the stage; and in the presence of fellow-actors who may be momentarily destroying the reality of the action.

A dramatist prepares the characterization of his personages in such a way that it will take advantage of the actor's gift.

Characterization in a novel is presented by the author's dogmatic assertion that the personage was such, and by an analysis of the personage with generally an account of his or her past. Since in the drama, this is replaced by the actual presence of the personage before us and since there is no occasion for the intervening all-knowing author to instruct us as to his or her inner nature, a far greater share is given in a play to (1) highly characteristic utterances and (2) concrete occasions in which the character defines itself under action and (3) a conscious preparation of the text whereby the actor may build upon the suggestions in the rôle according to his own abilities.

Characterization in a play is like a blank check which the dramatist accords to the actor for him to fill in—not entirely blank, for a number of indications of individuality are already there, but to a far less definite and absolute degree than in the novel.

The dramatist's principal interest being the movement of the story, he is willing to resign the more detailed aspects of characterization to the actor and is often rewarded beyond his expectation.

The sleep-walking scene from *Macbeth* is a highly compressed selection of words whereby despair and remorse rise to the surface of indirect confession. It is to be assumed that had Shakespeare lived to see what the genius of Sarah Siddons could pour into the scene from that combination of observation, self-knowledge, imagination and representational skill, even he might have exclaimed, "I never knew I wrote so well!"

II. THE THEATER IS AN ART ADDRESSED TO A GROUP-MIND.

Painting, sculpture, and the literature of the book are certainly solitary experiences; and it is likely that most people would agree that the audience seated shoulder to shoulder in a concert hall is not an essential element in musical enjoyment.

But a play presupposes a crowd. The reasons for this go deeper than (1) the economic necessity for the support of the play and (2) the fact that the temperament of actors is proverbially dependent on group attention.

It rests on the fact that (1) the pretense, the fiction, on the stage would fall to pieces and absurdity without the support accorded to it by a crowd, and (2) the excitement induced by pretending a fragment of life is such that it partakes of ritual and festival, and requires a throng.

Similarly the fiction that royal personages are of a mysteriously different nature from other people requires audiences, levées, and processions for its maintenance. Since the beginnings of society, satirists have occupied themselves with the descriptions of kings and queens in their intimacy and delighted in showing how the prerogatives of royalty become absurd when the crowd is not present to extend to them the enhancement of an imaginative awe.

The theater partakes of the nature of festival. Life imitated is life raised to a higher power. In the case of comedy, the vitality of these pretended surprises, deceptions, and *contretemps* becomes so lively that before a spectator, solitary or regarding himself as solitary, the structure of so much event would inevitably expose the artificiality of the attempt and ring hollow and unjustified; and in the case of tragedy, the accumulation of woe and apprehension would soon fall short of conviction. All actors know the disturbing sensation of playing before a handful of spectators at a dress rehearsal or performance where only their interest in pure craftsmanship can barely sustain them. During the last rehearsals the phrase is often heard: "This play is hungry for an audience."

Since the theater is directed to a group-mind, a number of consequences follow:

1. A group-mind presupposes, if not a lowering of standards, a broadening of the fields of interest. The other arts may presuppose an audience of connoisseurs trained in leisure and capable of being interested in certain rarefied aspects of life. The dramatist may be prevented from exhibiting, for example, detailed representations of certain moments in history that require specialized knowledge in the audience, or psychological states in the personages which are of insufficient general interest to evoke self-identification in the majority. In the Second Part of Goethe's *Faust* there are long passages dealing with the theory of paper money. The exposition of the nature of misanthropy (so much more drastic than Molière's) in Shakespeare's *Timon of Athens* has never been a success. The dramatist accepts this limitation in subject-matter and realizes that the group-mind imposes upon him the necessity of treating material understandable by the larger number.

2. It is the presence of the group-mind that brings another requirement to the theater—forward movement.

Maeterlinck said that there was more drama in the spectacle of an old man seated by a table than in the majority of plays offered to the public. He was juggling with the various meanings in the word "drama." In the sense whereby drama means the intensified concentration of life's diversity and significance he may well have been right; if he meant drama as a theatrical representation before an audience he was wrong. Drama on the stage is inseparable from forward movement, from action.

Many attempts have been made to present Plato's dialogues, Gobineau's fine series of dialogues, *La Renaissance*, and the *Imaginary Conversations* of Landor; but without success. Through some ingredient in the group-mind, and through the sheer weight of anticipation involved in the dressing-up and the assumption of fictional rôles, an action is required, and an action that is more than a mere progress in argumentation and debate.

III. THE THEATER IS A WORLD OF PRETENSE.

It lives by conventions: a convention is an agreed-upon falsehood, a permitted lie.

Illustrations: Consider at the first performance of the *Medea*, the passage where Medea meditates the murder of her children. An anecdote from antiquity tells us that the audience was so moved by this passage that considerable disturbance took place.

The following conventions were involved:

1. Medea was played by a man.

2. He wore a large mask on his face. In the lip of the mask was an acoustical device for projecting the voice. On his feet he wore shoes with soles and heels half a foot high.

3. His costume was so designed that it conveyed to the audience, by convention: woman of royal birth and oriental origin.

4. The passage was in metric speech. All poetry is an "agreed-upon falsehood" in regard to speech.

5. The lines were sung in a kind of recitative. All opera involves this "permitted lie" in regard to speech.

Modern taste would say that the passage would convey much greater pathos if a woman "like Medea" had delivered it—with an uncovered face that exhibited all the emotions she was undergoing. For the Greeks, however, there was no pretense that Medea was on the stage. The mask, the costume, the mode of declamation, were a series of signs which the spectator interpreted and reassembled in his own mind. Medea was being re-created within the imagination of each of the spectators.

The history of the theater shows us that in its greatest ages the stage employed the greatest number of conventions. The stage is fundamental pretense and it thrives on the acceptance of that fact and in the multiplication of additional pretenses. When it tries to assert that the personages in the action "really are," really inhabit such and such rooms, really suffer such and such emotions, it loses rather than gains credibility. The modern world is inclined to laugh condescendingly at the fact that in the plays of Racine and Corneille the gods and heroes of antiquity were dressed like the courtiers under Louis XIV; that in the Elizabethan age scenery was replaced by placards notifying the audience of the location; and that a whip in the hand and a jogging motion of the body indicated that a man was on horseback in the Chinese theater; these devices did not spring from naïveté, however, but from the vitality of the public imagination in those days and from an instinctive feeling as to where the essential and where the inessential lay in drama.

The convention has two functions:

1. It provokes the collaborative activity of the spectator's imagination; and

2. It raises the action from the specific to the general. This second aspect is of even greater importance than the first.

If Juliet is represented as a girl "very like Juliet"—it was not merely a deference to contemporary prejudices that assigned this rôle to a boy in the Elizabethan age— moving about in a "real" house with marble staircases, rugs, lamps and furniture, the impression is irresistibly conveyed that these events happened to this one girl, in one place, at one moment in time. When the play is staged as Shakespeare intended it, the bareness of the stage releases the events from the particular and the experience of Juliet partakes of that of all girls in love, in every time, place and language.

The stage continually strains to tell this generalized truth and it is the element of pretense that reinforces it. Out of the lie, the pretense, of the theater proceeds a truth more compelling than the novel can attain, for the novel by its own laws is constrained to tell of an action that "once happened"—"once upon a time."

IV. THE ACTION ON THE STAGE TAKES PLACE IN A PERPETUAL PRESENT TIME.

Novels are written in the past tense. The characters in them, it is true, are represented as living moment by moment their present time, but the constant running commentary of the novelist ("Tess slowly descended into the valley"; "Anna Karenina laughed") inevitably conveys to the reader the fact that these events are long since past and over.

The novel is a past reported in the present. On the stage it is always now. This confers upon the action an increased vitality which the novelist longs in vain to incorporate into his work.

This condition in the theater brings with it another important element:

In the theater we are not aware of the intervening story teller. The speeches arise from the characters in an apparently pure spontaneity.

A *play is what takes place.*

A *novel is what one person tells us took place.*

A play visibly represents pure existing. A novel is what one mind, claiming to omniscience, asserts to have existed.

Many dramatists have regretted this absence of the narrator from the stage, with his point of view, his powers of analyzing the behavior of the characters, his ability to interfere and supply further facts about the past, about simultaneous actions not visible on the stage, and above *all* his function of pointing the moral and emphasizing the significance of the action. In some periods of the theater he has been present as chorus, or prologue and epilogue or as *raisonneur*. But surely this absence constitutes an additional force to the form, as well as an additional tax upon the writer's skill. It is the task of the dramatist so to coordinate his play, through the selection of episodes and speeches, that though he is himself not visible, his point of view and his governing intention will impose themselves on the spectator's attention, not as dogmatic assertion or motto, but as self-evident truth and inevitable deduction.

Imaginative narration—the invention of souls and destinies—is to a philosopher an all but indefensible activity.

Its justification lies in the fact that the communication of ideas from one mind to another inevitably reaches the point where exposition passes into illustration, into parable, metaphor, allegory and myth.

It is no accident that when Plato arrived at the height of his argument and attempted to convey a theory of knowledge and a theory of the structure of man's nature he passed over into story telling, into the myths of the Cave and the Charioteer; and that the great religious teachers have constantly had recourse to the parable as a means of imparting their deepest intuitions.

The theater offers to imaginative narration its highest possibilities. It has many pitfalls and its very vitality betrays it into service as mere diversion and the enhancement of insignificant matter; but it is well to remember that it was the theater that rose to the highest place during those epochs that aftertime has chosen to call "great ages" and that the Athens of Pericles and the reigns of Elizabeth, Philip II, and Louis XIV were also the ages that gave to the world the greatest dramas it has known.

ABOUT THE AUTHOR

Thornton Wilder was born in Madison, Wisconsin, where his father was editor of a newspaper. When Thornton was nine years old, his father became Consul General, first in Hong Kong, where the young boy spent part of a year attending a German school; on a later trip when the family rejoined Mr. Wilder—who had been reassigned to Shanghai—Thornton went for a year to an English mission boarding school in Cheefoo. Between the China sojourns and after, he prepared for Oberlin College at schools in California. Finishing the sophomore year at Oberlin, he went to Yale, taking out a year in 1918 to serve in the Coast Guard before receiving his A.B. from Yale in 1920. The next year he spent at the American Academy in Rome studying archeology. During the following seven years he taught French and was a House Master at Lawrenceville with a year's leave of absence to get an M.A. from Princeton in 1925.

In 1942 Thornton Wilder joined the Air Force as a captain and served in this country, in North Africa and Italy until 1945, rising to the rank of lieutenant colonel. His home is in Hamden, Connecticut, but he travels a great deal and spends a considerable part of his time abroad. He has taught at both the University of Chicago and Harvard, and has held seminars and given lectures at many foreign universities.

Mr. Wilder is a member of the National Institute and the American Academy of Arts and Letters, and was awarded its Gold Medal for Fiction in 1952. He is known as a scholar of the classic Spanish dramatist, Lope de Vega, working on the dating of his plays, and as a diligent and admiring student of the works of James Joyce and Gertrude Stein, about both of whom he has written and lectured.

Mr. Wilder's first novel, *The Cabala*, was published in 1926. Late in 1927 came *The Bridge of San Luis Rey*, which received the 1928 Pulitzer Prize, giving him an international reputation as a novelist. Other novels followed: *The Woman of Andros, Heaven's My Destination, The Ides of March*, and *The Eighth Day*.

At the same time Mr. Wilder had been writing plays, and two volumes of short plays were published—*The Angel That Troubled the Waters* and *The Long Christmas Dinner*. In 1938 the production of *Our Town* won the Pulitzer Prize, and was followed by *The Merchant of Yonkers. The Skin of Our Teeth* was awarded the Pulitzer Prize in 1942. Like *The Matchmaker, A Life in the Sun* was first presented at the Edinburgh Festival.